SR Supplements / 16

Printed in the
United States
of America

SR SUPPLEMENTS

Volume 16

Studies in the Book of Job

edited by Walter E. Aufrecht

Published for the Canadian Corporation for Studies in Religion/Corporation Canadienne des Sciences Religieuses by Wilfrid Laurier University Press

1985

Canadian Cataloguing in Publication Data

Main entry under title:

Studies in the Book of Job

(SR supplements ; 16)
Papers presented at the Forty-ninth Annual Meeting
of the Canadian Society of Biblical Studies,
May 1981.
Includes bibliographical references and indexes.
ISBN 0-88920-179-X.

1. Bible. O.T. Job − Criticism, interpretation,
etc. − Congresses. I. Aufrecht, Walter Emanuel,
1942- . II. Canadian Society of Biblical Studies.
III. Series.

BS1415.2.S77 1985   223′.106   C85-098075-5

Cover design by Michael Baldwin, MSIAD

Order from:
Wilfrid Laurier University Press
Wilfrid Laurier University
Waterloo, Ontario, Canada   N2L 3C5

TABLE OF CONTENTS

INTRODUCTION

The essays in this volume were presented originally at the Forty-ninth Annual Meeting of the Canadian Society of Biblical Studies in May 1981. They are the first in a continuing series devoted to the book of Job, and are printed substantially in the form in which they were first delivered.

Professor Ronald J. Williams, in an inaugural lecture, dealt with the major aspects of Joban research: new commentaries, near eastern backgrounds, textual criticism, language and vocabulary, literary criticism, irony and satire, dating and theological ideas. Professor Williams' programmatic essay brings together and evaluates a vast amount of research on Job produced in the last thirty years.

The remaining three essays develop themes presented in the inaugural lecture. Professor Peter C. Craigie, in dealing with near eastern backgrounds, discusses the impact of Ugaritic language and literature on Joban research. He cautions against the over-enthusiastic use of Ugaritic, and shows how and in what areas Ugaritic contributes to an understanding of Job.

Professor Claude E. Cox is concerned with the textual criticism of Job, primarily with regard to the Septuagint. He lucidly illustrates the problems, methods and goals of textual criticism in the context of the Greek of Job 34.

In the final essay, the present writer deals with the language and vocabulary of Job, illustrating the importance of Aramaic in biblical studies in general and Joban studies in particular.

The essays taken together attempt to present an overview of the current issues in Joban studies, especially but not exclusively, those involving textual matters. It is hoped that they will illuminate and stimulate others in their study of the text and interpretative tradition of the Book of Job.

Lethbridge, Alberta

November, 1982

ACKNOWLEDGMENTS

The editor is indebted to the following individuals for their help in the production of this book: Christene Lestuka and Charlene Sawatsky, who did the typing; Glenn Allan, Marlene Haddad and Peter Madany of The University of Lethbridge computing services, who provided the typescript and layout; and Professor Christopher Foley of the University of Saskatoon, who expertly guided the manuscript through bureaucratic channels.

This book has been published with the help of a grant from the Canadian Federation for the Humanities using funds provided by the Social Sciences and Humanities Research Council of Canada.

CONTRIBUTORS

Walter E. Aufrecht is Associate Professor of Religious
Studies and Chairman of the Programme in
Religious Studies, The University of Lethbridge,
Lethbridge, Alberta.

Claude E. Cox is Assistant Professor of Religious
Studies and Chairman of the Department of
Religion, Brandon University, Brandon, Manitoba.

Peter C. Craigie is Professor of Religious Studies
and Dean of the Faculty of Humanities, The
University of Calgary, Calgary, Alberta.

Ronald J. Williams is Professor Emeritus of Hebrew and
Egyptology, Department of Near Eastern Studies,
The University of Toronto, Toronto, Ontario.

CURRENT TRENDS IN THE STUDY OF THE BOOK OF JOB

RONALD J. WILLIAMS

INTRODUCTION

Just over a quarter of a century ago, in 1953, I had the honour to deliver the Presidential address to the Canadian Society of Biblical Studies on the theme of Theodicy which was to appear in print a few years later.[1] It is thus a privilege and pleasure to be invited to address the Society again and return to the subject of the Book of Job which for so many years has occupied my attention.

By coincidence it was also in 1953 that Curt Kuhl produced his comprehensive survey of critical studies on the Book of Job,[2] soon to be followed by a discussion of problems raised by the biblical work.[3] For this reason I have selected 1954 as the starting-point for this review. Not that other surveys have since been lacking. H.H. Rowley published a lecture on "The Book of Job and its Meaning,"[4] which, in his characteristic style, commented on the views of many writers. A lecture by James Barr appeared in the same journal under the title

---

[1]R.J. Williams, "Theodicy in the Ancient Near East," *Canadian Journal of Theology* 2 (1956) 14-26.

[2]C. Kuhl, "Neuere Literarkritik des Buches Hiob," *Theologische Rundschau* 21 (1953) 163-205, 257-317.

[3]C. Kuhl, "Vom Hiobbuche und seinen Problemen," *Theologische Rundschau* 22 (1954) 261-316.

[4]H.H. Rowley, "The Book of Job and its Meaning," *Bulletin of the John Rylands University Library of Manchester* 41 (1958) 167-207.

"The Book of Job and its Modern Interpreters."[5]   The second edition
of Claus Westermann's *Der Aufbau des Buches Hiob* contains an
historical survey of literature since 1956 by Jürgen Kegler,[6] but
unfortunately this was not included in the English translation of the
volume.

Very useful indeed is the recent monograph by Hans-Peter Müller
in which he undertakes a methodical review of the recent literature,
prefacing it with a brief outline of major developments from the end of
the eighteenth until the early years of the present century.[7]   This is a
valuable and wide-ranging examination of the many facets of Joban
studies.

For many years I offered a graduate seminar on Job and
maintained a card bibliography of the subject.   When pressure of other
duties necessitated my relinquishing this practice some years ago, the
total had already exceeded 1500!   As Miloš Bič of Prague commented
in a book review as long ago as 1964, there is "an unmanageable mass
of literature on Job."[8]   Just how great a mass had been produced in
the past couple of decades alone I had hardly realized when I
undertook this task, and it has been necessary to be very selective in
order to keep within the limits imposed on our space.

I. NEW COMMENTARIES

Several important commentaries have been produced since 1954.
In 1955, Jean Steinmann published *Le Livre de Job* in which he

---

[5]J. Barr, "The Book of Job and its Modern Interpreters," *Bulletin of
the John Rylands University Library of Manchester* 54 (1971-1972) 28-46.

[6]C.   Westermann, *Der Aufbau des Buches Hiob*, 2nd ed. (Stuttgart:
Calwer Verlag, 1977) 9-25.

[7]H.-P. Müller, *Das Hiobproblem: seine Stellung und Entstehung im
alten Orient und im Alten Testament* (Darmstadt: Wissenschaftliche
Buchgesellschaft, 1978).

[8]M. Bič, Review of A. Jepsen, *Das Buch Hiob und seine Deutung*
(Berlin: Evangelische Verlagsanstalt, 1963), in *Book List of The Society
for Old Testament Study* (1964) 46-47.

expresses real appreciation of the book as great literature.[9]   Although he accepts the essential unity of the work, he judges chapters 24 and 28, the Elihu Speeches (chapters 32-37) and the section on the ostrich (39:13-18, lacking in the Septuagint) to be secondary.   He argues that the Yahweh Speeches (chapters 38-41) and the Epilogue (42:7-17) are later additions by the original author, following the lead of Albin van Hoonacker,[10] and Edouard Paul Dhorme,[11] and hence recognizes that the work passed through more than one edition.   He also devotes some attention to glosses as the work of ancient exegetes.

Samuel Terrien was responsible for the commentary in the *Interpreter's Bible*.[12]   Three years later this was followed by an interpretative volume entitled *Job: Poet of Existence*.[13]   He combined the contents of both in a very useful commentary in French.[14]   In it he accepts the book as a literary unity and only considers the Elihu Speeches to be secondary.

Georg Fohrer's massive volume, *Das Buch Hiob*,[15] is crammed with detail and is by far the most thorough of modern commentaries on Job.   Fohrer sees the passages on Behemoth and Leviathan as later additions and thus argues for a single speech of Yahweh as genuine and essential to the work which concluded with a single reply by Job.   He does, however, regard the Elihu Speeches and chapter 24 as secondary and recognizes that the third cycle of the Dialogue is in disorder.   We

---

[9]J. Steinmann, *Le Livre de Job* (Paris: Editions du Cerf, 1955).

[10]A.V. van Hoonacker, "Une question touchant la composition du livre de Job," *Revue biblique* 20 (1903) 161-189.

[11]E.P. Dhorme, *Le Livre de Job* (Paris: Victor Lecoffre, 1926); Eng. trans., *A Commentary on the Book of Job* (London: Nelson, 1967).

[12]S.L. Terrien, "The Book of Job: Introduction and Exegesis," *Interpreter's Bible* 3 (1954) 877-1198.

[13]S.L. Terrien, *Job: Poet of Existence* (New York: Bobbs-Merrill, 1957).

[14]S.L. Terrien, *Job* (Neuchâtel: Delachaux & Niestlé, 1963).

[15]G. Fohrer, *Das Buch Hiob* (Gütersloh: Gerd Mohn, 1963).

shall discuss his novel view of the frame-story (chapters 1-2; 42:7-17) later.

Marvin Pope contributed the volume on Job to the *Anchor Bible* series to which he later made substantial additions.[16] For him, chapter 28 and the Elihu Speeches are later accretions and the unsatisfactory preservation of the third cycle of the Dialogue is recognized. The frame-story is an original folktale utilized by the poet. The Yahweh Speeches he accepts as genuine with the exception of the Behemoth and Leviathan sections. His commentary is characterized by the most extensive but at the same time most sensible use of Ugaritic.

A concise and informative commentary in Dutch was well under way from the pen of Clemens Epping, when his unexpected demise necessitated the completion of the volume a year later by J. T. Nelis.[17] This is a remarkably thorough work for its size, mainly exegetical, but covering a surprising range of materials. The final speech of Zophar is recognized as missing, chapter 28 as a later addition, and the Elihu Speeches of different authorship from the Dialogue.

Friedrich Horst was engaged in preparing a commentary for the *Biblischer Kommentar: Altes Testament* when his sudden death in 1962 left it completed only as far as chapter 18. Fortunately this much is now in print.[18] He, too, believed chapter 28 and the Elihu Speeches to be secondary. It is to be hoped that the remainder of the commentary can be finished on the basis of his notes.

H.H. Rowley, alas, did not live to see the appearance of his commentary in the *Century Bible* series.[19] In a relatively small compass he provided a wealth of detail. As always, Rowley was cautious and hence his own conclusions are moderately conservative. He did, however, reject the Elihu Speeches, the second of the Yahweh Speeches, and chapter 28, although he suggested that the latter may have been from the original poet's hand.

---

[16]M.H. Pope, *Job* (Garden City: Doubleday & Co., Inc., 1965); 3rd rev. ed. (1973).

[17]C. Epping and J.T. Nelis, *Job uit de grondtekst vertaald en uitgelegd* (Roermond: Romen, 1968).

[18]F. Horst, *Hiob* (Neukirchen-Vluyn: Verlag des Erziehungsvereins, 1969).

[19]H.H. Rowley, *Job* (London: Thomas Nelson, 1970).

The two-volume opus of Jean Lévêque, *Job et son Dieu*, also belongs in this category.[20] It is characterized by careful exegesis of the text and follows most scholars in regarding chapter 28 and the Elihu Speeches as later additions. The distinguishing feature of this large and comprehensive work is its special emphasis on the theological interpretation of the Book of Job.

A commentary written by Francis Andersen takes an extremely conservative position.[21] The whole of Job, save for a few glosses, is assumed to be a unity and to date to a period prior to 750 B.C. There is, however, much of value to be gleaned from this little volume.

Robert Gordis, after an earlier and well-received volume entitled *The Book of God and Man*,[22] finally produced the desired commentary.[23] Although also conservative in his treatment of the text, his broad scholarship and mature wisdom provide a rich and often original exegesis, while his felicitous style is a delight to read.

Finally, the same year witnessed the launching of a new commentary by Franz Hesse in the *Zürcher Bibelkommentare* series.[24] He accepts the frame-story as the ancient legend, only without the second scene in heaven, and regards the Satan as the hypostatization of the wrath of God. The Dialogue (chapters 3-31) is thought to be post-exilic, but the Elihu Speeches to be later intrusions. He believes that the original divine response was a wordless theophany and that the present Yahweh Speeches represent several later stages of development.

---

[20]J. Lévêque, *Job et son Dieu: Essai d'éxegèse et de théologie biblique*, 2 vols. (Paris: J. Gabalda, 1970).

[21]F.I. Andersen, *Job: An Introduction and Commentary* (London: Inter Varsity Press 1976).

[22]R. Gordis, *The Book of God and Man: A Study of Job* (Chicago: University of Chicago Press, 1965).

[23]R. Gordis, *The Book of Job: Commentary, New Translation and Special Studies* (New York: Jewish Theological Seminary of America, 1978).

[24]F. Hesse, *Hiob* (Zurich: Theologischer Verlag, 1978).

II. NEAR EASTERN BACKGROUND

The latter half of the thought-provoking little monograph by
Hartmut Gese is devoted to an examination of the theme of the Book
of Job against the background of Mesopotamian literature.[25]   In this
the development of the doctrine of reward and punishment as related to
moral behaviour is given special attention.

The well-known Mesopotamian texts which deal with the problem
of suffering or theodicy,[26] have now been supplemented by a new tablet
which has come to light at Ugarit.   Jean Nougayrol was responsible for
making available this Akkadian work which deals with the complaints
of a sufferer.[27]   Abandoned by the gods, the afflicted man remains
faithful to Marduk who finally restores him to health.   The similarity
to the familiar *ludlul bēl nēmeqi* is striking in many points.

This latter work is preserved in copies from the seventh century
B.C., but it was probably composed during the Cassite period.   The
cuneiform tablet upon which the   new text is written must be dated
to c. 1300 B.C., although both language and orthography point to a
date for the original of c. 1700 B.C. or slightly earlier.   Nougayrol
speculates that the two texts may have come from a common source.
Strangely this new text is not mentioned by Pope in the third edition
of his commentary.[28]

A fresh discussion by John Gray of the Near Eastern matrix from
which the Book of Job emerged pays particular attention to the new

---

[25]H. Gese, *Lehre und Wirklichkeit in der alten Weisheit: Studien zu
den Sprüchen Salomos und zu dem Buche Hiob* (Tübingen: J.C.B.
Mohr, 1958) 51-78.

[26]For a reliable translation of the two major works, see W.G.
Lambert, *Babylonian Wisdom Literature* (Oxford: Clarendon Press,
1960) 21-29.

[27]J. Nougayrol, "Choix de textes littéraires: 162.   (Juste) souffrant,"
Ugaritica 5 (1968) 265-273.

[28]M. Pope, *Job* (n. 16).

cuneiform text.[29] He underlines the fact that this work was found in Ugarit, a centre from which so many other features were derived by the biblical writers.

III. TEXTUAL CRITICISM

With respect to the Hebrew of the Book of Job, a couple of fragments were found among the great hoard recovered from Cave 4 at Qumran in 1952.[30] The probability is that they will prove of little value for textual studies; indeed, one belongs to an Aramaic version.[31]

In the case of the Greek translation of Job, we note that Harry Orlinsky produced an important study which appeared in seven installments.[32] In it he scrutinizes the character of the text of the Septuagint and classifies the translator's methods of rendering the Hebrew text into Greek. Thus he concludes that the resulting version does not necessarily imply a variant text in the Hebrew *Vorlage*. The translator frequently paraphrases for no apparent reason. This accounts in part for the fact that the Septuagint text is one-sixth shorter than the Hebrew.

Orlinsky also demonstrates that the common view of the Septuagint translator as "anti-anthropomorphic" is an exaggeration. Neither does the version reveal a consistent tendency to tone down "blasphemous" statements, in spite of the conclusions of Henry

---

[29]J. Gray, "The Book of Job in the Context of Near Eastern Literature," *Zeitschrift für die alttestamentliche Wissenschaft* 82 (1970) 251-269.

[30]B. Zuckerman, "Job, Book of," *Interpreter's Dictionary of the Bible, Supplementary Volume*, ed. K. Crim (Nashville: Abingdon Press, 1976) 479.

[31]J.T. Milik, "Targum de Job," *Discoveries in the Judean Desert IV, Qumrân Grotte 4, II* (Oxford: Clarendon Press, 1977) 90, plt. 28:157.

[32]H.M. Orlinsky, "Studies in the Septuagint of the Book of Job," *Hebrew Union College Annual* 28 (1957) 53-74; ibid., 29 (1958) 229-271; ibid., 30 (1959) 153-167; ibid., 32 (1961) 239-268; ibid., 33 (1962) 119-151; ibid., 35 (1964) 57-78; ibid., 36 (1965) 37-47.

Gehman,[33] and his student Donald Gard.[34]   Orlinsky contends that
Codex Vaticanus is the best witness to the Septuagint, although even it
contains corruptions.   As far as I am aware, the Göttingen Septuagint
Project edition of Job is still in press.

The Syriac text has a special value for textual criticism since it
was made directly from the Hebrew.   The late L.G. Rignell, who has
prepared the text of Job for the Leiden Peshiṭta Project, offered some
comments on the version in a brief article.[35]   He suspects that there
was more than one translator at work.

The Aramaic targum of Job, long known from its inclusion in the
Rabbinic Bibles, is usually thought to come from the fourth century
A.D.   A doctoral dissertation dealing with this targum was completed
in 1974 by Raphael Weiss.   After his premature death in the same
year, the thesis eventually appeared in print.[36]   His original intention of
producing a critical text was thwarted by the inadequacy of the
available source materials.   Despite this, however, he deals thoroughly
with the exegetical methods and special features of the targum.   His
view is that it was a compilation of various targums which were most
likely of different dates.

In 1956 fragments of a new targum were discovered in Qumran
Cave 11 which were published in 1971 by Jean van der Ploeg and
Adam van der Woude.[37]   Paleographically the fragments may be dated
to the early part of the first century A.D., but the grammatical forms
suggest that the original goes back to the late second century B.C.   A

---

[33]H.S. Gehman, "The Theological Approach of the Greek Translator
of Job 1-15," *Journal of Biblical Literature* 68 (1949) 231-240.

[34]D.H. Gard, *The Exegetical Method of the Greek Translator of the
Book of Job* (Philadelphia: Society of Biblical Literature, 1952);
reprinted (1967).

[35]L.G. Rignell, "Notes on the Peshiṭta of the Book of Job," *Annual
of the Swedish Theological Institute* 9 (1973) 98-106.

[36]R. Weiss, *The Aramaic Targum of the Book of Job* (Tel Aviv: Tel-
Aviv University, 1979), (in Hebrew with English summary).

[37]J.P.M. van der Ploeg and A.S. van der Woude *Le targum de Job
de la grotte XI de Qumrân* (Leiden: E.J. Brill, 1971).

new edition supplementing this one was the work of Michael Sokoloff and was largely of a linguistic nature.[38] In the same year a valuable article by Joseph Fitzmyer made its appearance,[39] and John Gray assessed the significance of the new targum with respect to the Massoretic text, the previously-known targum and the Septuagint.[40]

Despite the fragmentary condition of the Qumran targum, preserving only portions of chapters 17 to 42, it is still extremely important as a witness to the form of the text at about the time when the Septuagint version was made. The preserved sections prove that the controversial chapter 24 and the disturbed order of the third cycle of the Dialogue were already in their present form along with chapter 28, Job's monologue in chapters 29-31, the Elihu Speeches in chapters 32-37, and the Yahweh Speeches in chapters 38-41 (including, be it noted, the pericopes on Behemoth and Leviathan!), as well as the closing words of Job and the Epilogue. However, the targum ends at 42:11 in the middle of the line, leaving the remainder of the scroll blank.

IV. LANGUAGE AND VOCABULARY

The language of Job has also contributed to the difficulties of the book, permeated as it is with numerous unusual expressions and *hapax legomena*, a fact that has led some scholars to claim that the Hebrew is a translation. Thus, in 1926, Robert Pfeiffer had argued for the

---

[38]M. Sokoloff, *The Targum to Job from Qumran Cave XI* (Ramat-Gan: Bar-Ilan University, 1974).

[39]J. Fitzmyer, "Some Observations on the Targum of Job from Qumran Cave 11," *The Catholic Biblical Quarterly* 36 (1974) 503-524; reprinted in J.A. Fitzmyer, *A Wandering Aramean, Collected Aramaic Essays* (Missoula: Scholars Press, 1979) 161-182.

[40]J. Gray, "The Massoretic Text of the Book of Job, the Targum and the Septuagint Version in the Light of the Qumran Targum (11 Qtarg Job)," *Zeitschrift für die alttestamentliche Wissenschaft* 86 (1974) 331-350.

Edomite origin of the work.[41]   In 1941 Harry Torczyner (Tur-Sinai) claimed that the book was in part translated from Aramaic,[42] but he gained few supporters.

Earlier still, Arabic had been suggested as the original language of the book,[43] and following this lead an article by Alfred Guillaume proposed north Arabia as the home of the work.[44]   This was later to be elaborated in a monograph which appeared posthumously.[45]   This theory too has failed to achieve general acceptance.   However, the Arabic language has for long been regarded as an inexhaustible mine for etymological speculation and was much exploited by Sir Godfrey Driver in a series of lexicographical articles.[46]   It must be admitted that only a small percentage of his suggestions has met with favour.

For obvious reasons, contributions from Ugaritic tend to be much more acceptable.   The most active worker in this area was the late Mitchell Dahood who produced a spate of articles beginning in 1952 in which he sought to explain, with a minimum of emendation, obscure

---

[41]R.H.   Pfeiffer,   "Edomitic   Wisdom,"   *Zeitschrift   für   die alttestamentliche Wissenschaft* 44 (1926) 13-25.

[42]N.H. Torczyner, *The Book of Job* (Jerusalem: Hebrew University Press, 1941); N.H.   Tur-Sinai, *The Book of Job: A New Commentary* (Jerusalem: Kiryath Sepher, 1957) xxx-xl.

[43]F.H.   Foster, "Is the Book of Job a Translation from an Arabic Original?"   *American Journal of Semitic Languages and Literatures* 49 (1932-1933) 21-45.

[44]A.   Guillaume, "The Arabic Background of the Book of Job," *Promise and Fulfilment: Essays Presented to S.H. Hooke,* ed. F.F. Bruce (Edinburgh: T.& T. Clark, 1963) 106-127.

[45]A.   Guillaume, *Studies in the Book of Job,* ed. J. MacDonald (Leiden: E.J. Brill, 1968).

[46]See for example, G.R.   Driver, "Problems in the Hebrew Text of Job," *Vetus Testamentum Supplements* 3 (1955) 72-93.

words and problematical verses.[47] Not infrequently, it must be confessed, there is some difficulty in seeing wherein the problem lies; but this is also a criticism of many of Driver's etymologies. Nevertheless, Dahood's influence has been considerable. Anton Blommerde, a pupil of his, published a thesis entitled *Northwest Semitic Grammar and Job*.[48] Marvin Pope, in his valuable commentary on Job, has made extensive and reasonable use of Ugaritic.[49]

There is, to be sure, a constant danger of overenthusiasm, which often may result in unfortunate excesses. In a lecture delivered in 1972, James Barr warned against the abuses arising from the uncontrolled use of Ugaritic, making special reference to Job.[50] Stimulated by Barr's judicious and sobering remarks in the volume *Comparative Philology and the Text of the Old Testament*,[51] Lester Grabbe completed a doctoral thesis in 1975, which was subsequently published.[52] In this he examined fifty passages in Job for which new etymologies had been proposed in order to test the validity of the methods employed. These studies demonstrate the importance of rigid standards in determining possible cognates.

---

[47]M. Dahood, "Some Northwest Semitic words in Job," *Biblica* 38 (1957) 306-320; idem, "Northwest Semitic Philology and Job," *The Bible in Current Catholic Thought*, ed. J.L. McKenzie (New York: Herder and Herder, 1962) 55-74; idem, "Some Rare Parallel Word Pairs in Job and in Ugaritic," *The Word in the World*, ed. R.J. Clifford and G.W. MacRae (Weston, Mass.: Weston College Press, 1973) 19-34.

[48]A.C.M. Blommerde, *Northwest Semitic Grammar and Job* (Rome: Pontifical Biblical Institute, 1969).

[49]M. Pope, *Job* (n. 16).

[50]J. Barr, "Philology and Exegesis: Some General Remarks, with Illustrations from Job," *Questions disputées d'Ancien Testament*, ed. C. Brekelmans (Gembloux: Leuven University, 1974) 39-61.

[51]J. Barr, *Comparative Philology and the Text of the Old Testament* (Oxford: Clarendon Press, 1968).

[52]L.L. Grabbe, *Comparative Philology and the Text of Job: A Study in Methodology* (Missoula: Scholars Press, 1977).

V. LITERARY CRITICISM

Literary criticism, as distinct from textual criticism, should concern itself with features of style as well as with figures of speech and word-plays. We shall have occasion to consider some of these factors in the course of our discussion. The principles of prosody are also relevant to the subject, so we shall begin with them.

The presence of strophic structure in the Dialogue of the Book of Job had been championed as early as 1946, when William Irwin devoted an article to it.[53]   Fifteen years later Patrick Skehan advanced an alternative scheme,[54] to which he returned once more.[55]   Samuel Terrien employed a structure not unlike that of Irwin in his later commentary.[56]   The value of such a structure is apparent not only in the enhanced appreciation of the poetic form, but also on occasion in the indication of whether verses may be original or secondary additions.

Still other literary features, such as doublets or contradictions, may likewise prove valuable in determining the presence of different sources or of secondary material.   By employing criteria such as these the majority of scholars by the mid-'fifties regarded the Book of Job as consisting of a number of units of varying degrees of homogeneity or authenticity.   The scholarly consensus recognizes the following sections: (1) Prose Prologue, chapters 1-2 (some parts possibly later than others); (2) Dialogue, chapters 3-27 (the third cycle of speeches in confusion); (3) Wisdom Hymn, chapter 28; (4) Job's Monologue, chapters 29-31; (5) Elihu Speeches, chapters 32-37 (four speeches, perhaps by different authors); (6) Yahweh Speeches with Job's Responses, chapters 38:1-42:6 (uncertainty prevails as to whether there are two speeches or only one, and one reply by Job or two); (7) Prose Epilogue, chapter 42:7-17

---

[53]W.A. Irwin, "Poetic Structure in the Dialogue of Job," *Journal of Near Eastern Studies* 5 (1946) 26-39.

[54]P.W. Skehan, "Strophic Patterns in the Book of Job," *The Catholic Biblical Quarterly* 23 (1961) 129-143.

[55]P.W. Skehan, "Job's Final Plea (Job 29-31) and the Lord's Reply (Job 38-41)," *Biblica* 45 (1964) 51-62.

[56]S.L. Terrien, *Job* (n. 14).

(whether this forms part of the Prologue or is separate is a matter of controversy).

It might indeed be said that there is hardly any permutation or combination of arrangements of these materials or assessments of genuineness or spuriousness of passages or sections that has not been advanced by some commentator. This chaotic situation led Otto Eissfeldt to declare that the literary analysis of the Book of Job "is much more dependent upon the interpretation of the book, based upon intuitive understanding, than is the case with other books, and so to a much greater degree at the mercy of subjective feelings and personal taste."[57]

The frame-story (chapters 1-2, 42:7-17) has been the subject of much discussion in recent years. Do the Prologue and Epilogue belong together? Was it an ancient folktale? If so, was it oral or written? These are some of the many questions that have been raised. Scholars have been divided over whether it was a written account used by the poet or whether the present frame-story was a prose retelling of the earlier folktale by the poet. Tur-Sinai in 1957 even regarded the present frame-story as a later addition to the work which replaced an older frame-story.[58] Furthermore, most scholars were inclined to view the Epilogue as a later appendage.

In an important article, Nahum Sarna insisted that both Prologue and Epilogue were from the same hand.[59] He carefully pointed out how features such as repetition, schematic structure and mythological motifs all point to an epic style similar to that of the Ugaritic poems and consequently argue for an early date. Indeed, as he observed, an epic of Job is clearly implied by Ezekiel 14:14, 20.

---

[57]O. Eissfeldt, *The Old Testament: An Introduction*, trans. P.R. Ackroyd (New York: Harper & Row, 1965) 456.

[58]N.H. Tur-Sinai, *The Book of Job: A New Commentary* (n. 42).

[59]N.M. Sarna, "Epic Substratum in the Prose of Job," *Journal of Biblical Literature* 76 (1957) 13-25.

An article by Georg Fohrer advanced arguments in favour of accepting the frame-story as an earlier work which the poet used.[60] In his monumental commentary, he incorporates the theory developed in the article of at least four stages of growth:[61] (1) a pre-Israelite tale in which Job is portrayed as a semi-nomadic Edomite and the episode of the heavenly court is described but without the Satan. Then, (2) an early pre-exilic version, produced in the ninth to eight centuries B.C., was marked by the epic style described by Sarna, adding such features as camels and the patriarchal parallels. Next, (3) in the early exilic period still further additions took place, including the Deuteronomic phraseology. And finally, (4) in the post-exilic period, the figure of the Satan was introduced as well as some features of wisdom teaching.

In an article that appeared in the same year as his commentary,[62] Fohrer pointed out striking parallels between the frame-story and the Prayer of Nabonidus, which had been discovered in Qumran Cave 4 in 1956.[63] Hence, he concluded that the frame-story is not by the author of the poem but was adapted and modified by him for his own purposes. The three friends, for instance, take over the function of the relatives of Job in the original form of the folktale.

As has long been observed, the Job of the Prologue is a model of the patient, pious sufferer (cf. James 5:11), whereas in the Dialogue he is depicted as an angry man in open revolt. This contradictory situation is explained by H.L. Ginsberg in a daring article.[64] In it he postulates an original work consisting of Job 1:1-2:13, after which a

---

[60]G. Fohrer, "Überlieferung und Wandlung der Hioblegende," *Hebräische Wortforschung*, ed. L. Rost (Erlangen: Universitätsbibliothek, 1959) 41-62; reprinted in G. Fohrer, *Studien zum Buche Hiob* (Gütersloh: Gerd Mohn, 1963) 44-67.

[61]G. Fohrer, *Das Buch Hiob* (n. 15).

[62]G. Fohrer, "4QOrNab, 11QtgJob und die Hioblegende," *Zeitschrift für die alttestamentliche Wissenschaft* 75 (1963) 93-97.

[63]J.T. Milik, "'Prière de Nabonide' et autres écrits d'un cycle de Daniel," *Revue biblique* 63 (1956) 407-411.

[64]H.L. Ginsberg, "Job the Patient and Job the Impatient," *Conservative Judaism* 21 (1967) 12-28; reprinted in *Vetus Testamentum Supplements* 17 (1969) 88-111.

section now absent from the text is assumed to portray the friends as following the lead of Job's wife in counselling Job to reject so cruel a God. This was immediately succeeded by chapters 27-28, in which Job counters his friends' heresy. Possibly a further missing section came next, in which the Deity commended Job's words. The whole concluded with 42:7-17 describing the divine rebuke of the friends and the rewarding of Job. What we possess in chapters 3-42 (omitting chapters 27-28) is the later work of a great poet who reverses the roles of Job and his friends.

In a small monograph Hans-Peter Müller employs the criteria of traditio-historical criticism in an attempt to determine from earlier Near Eastern literature as well as later haggadic sources the original form of the legend of Job.[65]   He begins with the second century A.D. Testament of Job, newly edited by Sebastian Brock.[66]   This is a paraphrase of earlier Hebrew traditions in which the friends clearly make accusations against Job who is just as clearly blameless in his demeanour.   It is also in complete agreement with Job 42:7-8 where Yahweh says to Eliphaz, "My wrath is kindled against you and your two friends, for you have not spoken what is right about me as my servant Job has." The study emphasizes the underlying difference in the portrayal of Job and his friends in the poetic Dialogue from that in the pre-biblical legend. Müller shows how similar Jewish traditions survived in Arabic literature in the writings of such authors as At-Ṭabarī and Ath-Thaʿlabī of the eleventh century. In fact, this had already been noted by Duncan Macdonald in the last century.[67]

As we have already noted, the Job Targum from Qumran clearly shows that the end of the Epilogue, 42:12-17, formed no part of the text it rendered, so that these verses may well have been part of the process of midrashic accretions which continued into the version of the Septuagint.

---

[65]H.-P. Müller, *Hiob und seine Freunde* (Zurich: EVZ-Verlag, 1970).

[66]S.P. Brock, *Testamentum Jobi* (Leiden: E.J. Brill, 1967).

[67]D.B. Macdonald, "Some External Evidence on the Original Form of the Legend of Job," *American Journal of Semitic Languages and Literatures* 14 (1897-1898) 137-164.

Another section of the book which has been the object of some discussion is the Elihu Speeches. These are still regarded by most scholars as later additions to the work. Robert Gordis, however, in *The Book of God and Man*,[68] and in his new commentary stoutly maintains that they, together with chapter 28, were written by the poet of the Dialogue in his later years.[69]

Norman Snaith also views them as the latest creation of the same author. In his little volume *The Book of Job*,[70] if we may digress for a moment, Snaith visualizes the Book of Job as being composed in three stages by the one author. (1) The frame-story (1:1-2:10 and 42:10-16) enclosed Job's soliloquy (chapters 3, 29-31), the Yahweh Speeches (chapters 38-39, 40:6-41:26) and Job's responses (40:1-5, 42:1-6). (2) The friends were introduced into the Prologue (2:11-13), and then the Dialogue (chapters 4-27) was inserted into Job's soliloquy along with some practical advice offered in chapter 28. (3) In order to reinforce the concluding advice in 28:28, "To fear Yahweh is wisdom; to depart from evil is understanding," the Elihu Speeches were then introduced as the "crown" of the work, a view held much earlier by Karl Budde,[71] and Carl Cornill.[72]

In an earlier article Georg Fohrer examined the Elihu Speeches and discerned a common structure in three of them.[73] Hence he found it probable that they should be ascribed to a common author. He believes the latter to be a sage who contradicts the friends' claim that Job's sufferings were the result of common human failings and

---

[68]R. Gordis, *The Book of God and Man* (n. 22).

[69]R. Gordis, *The Book of Job* (n. 23).

[70]N.H. Snaith, *The Book of Job: Its Origin and Purpose* (London: S.C.M. Press, 1968).

[71]K. Budde, *Das Buch Hiob* (Göttingen: Vandenhoek & Ruprecht, 1896).

[72]C.H. Cornill, *Einleitung in das Alte Testament* (Tübingen: J.C.B. Mohr, 1891).

[73]G. Fohrer, "Die Weisheit des Elihu (Hi 32-37)," *Archiv für Orientforschung* 19 (1959-1960) 83-94; reprinted in *Studien zum Buche Hiob* (n. 60) 87-107.

shortcomings or justly deserved punishment. Rather did they serve a salutary and admonitory purpose, since God was seeking man's welfare.

David Noel Freedman also devoted an article to the Elihu Speeches.[74] The seemingly unnecessary division into four speeches led him to the speculation that they may have been designed, perhaps by the original author of the Book of Job, for insertion at appropriate points in the Dialogue. He came to this conclusion because the speeches make frequent reference to the Dialogue and even quote from it. Freedman proposes that they may have been intended to conclude each cycle of speeches and Job's final monologue, but that the plan was abandoned when the Yahweh Speeches were composed, using some of the same material. Finally, an editor preserved the Elihu Speeches by inserting them in their present position.

The view propounded by Georg Fohrer with respect to the Yahweh Speeches deserves some attention.[75] He argues that a reply by the Deity to Job is an essential part of the composition, but that there was but one speech of the Lord and one response by Job in the original work. He regards the Behemoth and Leviathan passages (40:15-41:26 [Eng. 34]) as later additions, so that the original Yahweh Speech comprised 38:2-39:30; 40:2, 8-14. Job's answer is found in 40:4-5; 42:2-3 (omitting 3a), 5-6.

Although it is legitimate and indeed essential to distinguish the various components of a literary work and to determine their purpose and message if at all possible, this is not the end of the task for the biblical interpreter. It is also necessary to view the work as a whole in its present form. This is certainly true from the standpoint of literary appreciation, as Northrop Frye has long insisted.[76] But it is no less valid from the standpoint of religious or theological understanding. This has been well argued by Brevard Childs in his *Introduction to the*

---

[74]D.N. Freedman, "The Elihu Speeches in the Book of Job," *Harvard Theological Review* 61 (1968) 51-59.

[75]G. Fohrer, "Gottes Antwort aus dem Sturmwind (Hi 38-41)," *Theologische Zeitschrift* 18 (1962) 1-24; reprinted in *Studien zum Buche Hiob* (n. 60) 108-129.

[76]See most recently, H.N. Frye, *The Great Code: The Bible and Literature* (Toronto: Academic Press, 1981).

Old Testament as Scripture.[77] Unfortunately, our use of terms such as "secondary," "later," and "spurious" implies a pejorative connotation that has blinded us to the fact that these works, with whatever accretions they may have acquired, were the product of the Hebrew religious community and became part of canonical Scripture in the form in which we have them. It is most gratifying to see that this is the trend of much of biblical criticism today.

VI. IRONY AND SATIRE

Such fruitful insights have been made possible by attention to the literary device of irony that it has seemed proper to devote a special section to it. Roderick MacKenzie advanced the view that the answer to Job's problem is developed in the Yahweh Speeches by means of irony.[78] For him the key passage is 40:8, "Will you even put me in the wrong? Will you condemn me to justify yourself?" These words addressed to Job suggest that Yahweh is ironically inquiring of Job whether he is a rival god. Both Job and the friends had proclaimed the divine power, the friends stressing divine justice and Job complaining of omnipotent caprice. The Yahweh Speeches emphasize not only the power of the Deity, but also his providence and love. Retribution is therefore irrelevant to the situation.

In 1961 a doctoral dissertation dealing with the theme of irony in the Book of Job was completed by William Power under my supervision, but unfortunately remains unpublished.[79] In it he discussed the several types of irony: verbal, dramatic, and cosmic. He went on to illustrate the uses of irony in the Dialogue and demonstrated its value in confirming the authenticity of some passages generally regarded

---

[77]B. Childs, *Introduction to the Old Testament as Scripture* (Philadelphia: Fortress Press, 1979).

[78]R.A.F. MacKenzie, "The Purpose of the Yahweh Speeches in the Book of Job," *Biblica* 40 (1959) 435-445; reprinted in *Studia Biblica et Orientalia*, I (Analecta Biblica 10), (Rome: Biblical Institute Press, 1959) 301-311.

[79]W.J.A. Power, "A Study of Irony in the Book of Job," (Ph.D. diss., University of Toronto, 1961).

as later additions.   For instance, ironic word-plays reveal that the poet
of the Dialogue knew the Prologue in its present form, including the
Satan passages.

A brief article in *The Personalist* by Gerald Larue makes the
startling assertion that the Book of Job was designed to show that
theological argument is an exercise in futility for the resolution of Job's
problem.[80]   He even hints slyly that the poet had his tongue in cheek.

In 1965 a volume on *Irony in the Old Testament* by Edwin Good
made its appearance, and it has recently been reissued in a second
edition.[81]   Chapter 7 was entitled "Job: The Irony of Reconciliation."
In it he shows how, through the medium of irony, the poet frequently
reverses the meaning of certain expressions.   Like Fr. MacKenzie, he
regards 40:8 as a key verse.   For him, this expresses the irony of Job's
position *vis à vis* God.   Job's claim to deserve justification is the nub
of the problem: his exposing of his view of justice to that of God.
Basically, Good sees the work as a struggle between magic (i.e., man's
attempt to force divine favour by good works) and faith.

An important article by Matitiahu Tsevat on "The Meaning of the
Book of Job" deserves serious consideration.[82]   In it he points out that
Job rejects his friends' insistence that since, in their view, sin provokes
punishment and virtue brings reward, the corollary also holds true, viz.,
that suffering always implies sin.   The poet's answer, then, is to deny
any principle of retributive justice.   This concept of an amoral universe
might imply indifference on the part of the Deity.   But, in the Book of
Job, God is not indifferent.   Does this mean that God is himself
amoral or even unjust?   Whatever Tsevat's own attitude may be,
biblical theology has always maintained the principle of divine   חן ,
"grace," which is not dependent on man's deserts but on God's loving
favour.

Tsevat also claims that Job forces God's hand and makes God
respond to his challenge by the oath in chapter 31.   That is why God

---

[80]G.A. Larue, "The Book of Job on the Futility of Theological
Discussion," *The Personalist* 45 (1964) 72-79.

[81]E.M. Good, *Irony in the Old Testament* (Philadelphia: Westminster
1965); 2nd ed. (Sheffield: The Almond Press, 1981).

[82]M. Tsevat, "The Meaning of the Book of Job," *Hebrew Union
College Annual* 37 (1966) 73-106.

reveals himself. Yet the theophany is itself his vindication, for the Deity reveals himself only to the pious, according to Job's own words in 13:16, "This will be my salvation, that a godless man shall not come before Him."

From the pen of James Williams comes an article with the title "Mystery and Irony in Job."[83] Like Tsevat, he views the author of the Book of Job as questioning the retributive justice assumed in both the folktale and the Dialogue and portraying God as amoral caprice. He examines the tension between the frame-story on one hand and the Yahweh Speeches on the other. This tension produced an irony that can be elucidated by the insights of Jung,[84] according to Williams. God rather than Job is on trial!

In 1973 David Robertson contributed an important paper to *Soundings* in which he makes a literary study of the book as a whole except for chapter 28 and the Elihu Speeches.[85] He shows how irony pervades the whole work. Like Williams, he sees God as incriminating himself; but he has an even more convincing conclusion: "God is the friends writ large." That is to say, we have a parody! He accepts Tsevat's opinion of the significance of Job's oath.

This paper is accompanied by a response from Edwin Good.[86] He observes that justice, in the sense of reward and punishment, is not part of the cosmic order. In the final speeches Yahweh shifts the issue from Job's question of justice to the question of order. Good also notes that there was no actual wager between God and the Satan, but suggests that it was the latter's oath (which, of course, involved a self-curse) that gave rise to the whole plot.

---

[83]J.G. Williams, "'You have not spoken Truth of Me': Mystery and Irony in Job," *Zeitschrift für die alttestamentliche Wissenschaft* 83 (1971) 231-255.

[84]C.G. Jung, *Antwort auf Hiob* (Zurich: Rascher, 1952); Eng. trans. (New York: Meridian, 1960).

[85]D.A. Robertson, "The Book of Job: A Literary Study," *Soundings* 56 (1973) 446-469.

[86]E.M. Good, "Job and the Literary Task: A Response," *Soundings* 56 (1973) 470-484.

A novel approach was offered by William Whedbee in the 1977 number of *Semeia*, which was devoted entirely to the Book of Job.[87] He championed an interpretation of the complete book in its present form as a comedy. Here the term "comedy" is employed in the strict sense of a literary form characterized by the presence of irony and incongruity and also providing a happy conclusion. He sees the work as filled with irony, sarcasm, parodies, and *double entendre.* Even the figure of Elihu serves to contribute "comic relief." He believes that the Epilogue is essential to the work as comedy, since restoration and a harmonious resolution are required.

In the same periodical James Williams furnishes some helpful comments on Whedbee's paper and stresses the role of Job as an intercessor.[88] At this point, I think it needs to be emphasized that what may seem to be impiety to some readers of these studies is actually intended as a literary judgment on the form of presentation and the devices employed by the Hebrew poet to accomplish his task.

Along a somewhat similar line is the volume by Dermot Cox entitled *The Triumph of Impotence: Job and the Tradition of the Absurd.*[89] In it, he compares the Book of Job with the works of Camus, Beckett, Kafka, and the like in the Comedy of the Absurd. The parallels are indicated as Job cries out for death and release from meaningless misery. The "triumph" of the biblical work is found in the concluding theophany, which transcends Job's dilemma and thus progresses beyond the theatre of the absurd.

In 1977 there appeared a book with the title *Biblical Structuralism* in which Robert Polzin employed what has been called the "new criticism," that is to say, the application of structural analysis to the

---

[87]J.W. Whedbee, "The Comedy of Job," *Studies in the Book of Job, Semeia* 7 (Missoula: Scholars Press, 1977) 1-39.

[88]J.G. Williams, "Comedy, Irony, Intercession: A Few Notes in Response," *Studies in the Book of Job, Semeia* 7 (Missoula: Scholars Press, 1977) 135-145.

[89]D. Cox, *The Triumph of Impotence: Job and the Tradition of the Absurd* (Rome: Universita Gregoriana, 1978).

Book of Job.[90]   This expands on a brief article in *Interpretation.*[91]   He shows how the work may be seen as a careful balancing of contradiction and inconsistency.   This produces tensions which constitute what he describes as a spiritual journey from "equilibrium without insight to equilibrium with insight," achieved by "the integration of contradiction and resolution."   I fear this will not be easily or readily grasped by many readers, and by its very nature the method is so highly subjective that it imposes a strain on one's credulity.

VII. DATING

The commonly accepted date for the Book of Job in its present form has been the fourth century B.C., although Georg Fohrer prefers a less restricted period, suggesting some time between the fifth and third centuries.[92]   The tendency in recent years has been to push it back somewhat earlier.   Jean Lévêque   has recently argued for the completion of the work in the first half of the fifth century.[93]

Crucial to the dating of the whole book is the dating of the Dialogue.   It was Thomas Cheyne who first put forward the opinion that the Dialogue had been produced earlier than the writings of Deutero-Isaiah.[94]   This view was adopted by Robert Pfeiffer in a brief

---

[90]R.M. Polzin, *Biblical Structuralism: Method and Subjectivity in the Study of Ancient Texts* (Missoula: Scholars Press, 1977).

[91]R.M. Polzin, "The Framework of the Book of Job," *Interpretation* 28 (1974) 182-200.

[92]G. Fohrer, *Das Buch Hiob* (n. 15) 42.

[93]J. Lévêque,   "La datation du livre de Job," *Vetus Testamentum Supplements* 32 (1981) 206-219.

[94]T.K. Cheyne, *The Prophecies of Isaiah*, II (London: Kegan Paul & Trench, 1882) 252.

article,[95] and also by Marvin Pope in his commentary,[96] as well as by Samuel Terrien in his commentaries.[97] The latter subsequently offered evidence that Deutero-Isaiah seems to be responding to some of Job's questions concerning human existence.[98] Since the poet of the Dialogue appears to have modelled Job's lament in chapter 3 on Jeremiah 20:14-18, Terrien regards 580-540 B.C. as a likely period for its composition.

Much more drastic is the date proposed by David Robertson in his doctoral thesis, which was completed in 1966 and published a few years later.[99] Based on a study of a number of linguistic features, he claims to be able to give a relative dating to Hebrew poetry. In the case of the poetry of the Book of Job, he argues in favour of the tenth or even eleventh century B.C.[100]

A study by David Noel Freedman is devoted to the orthographic practices of the text of Job.[101] The occurrence of many contracted diphthongs betrays a feature of the pre-exilic northern Israelite dialect as distinct from that of Jerusalem. A date for the production of the book in the Israelite diaspora during the seventh or early sixth century B.C. is advocated. Frank Moore Cross believes that there is evidence that early material was reworked by the poet in the sixth century

---

[95]R.H. Pfeiffer, "The Priority of Job over Is. 40-55," *Journal of Biblical Literature* 46 (1927) 202-206.

[96]M. Pope, *Job* (1965) xxxiii; (1973) xl (n. 16).

[97]S.L. Terrien, "The Book of Job" (n. 12) 889-890; idem, *Job* (n. 14) 23-24.

[98]S.L. Terrien, "Quelques remarques sur les affinités de Job avec le Deutéro-Esaïe," *Vetus Testamentum Supplements* 15 (1966) 295-310.

[99]D.A. Robertson, *Linguistic Evidence in Dating Early Hebrew Poetry* (Philadelphia: Society of Biblical Literature, 1972).

[100]Ibid., 155.

[101]D.N. Freedman, "Orthographic Peculiarities in the Book of Job," *Eretz-Israel* 9 (1969) 35-44.

B.C.[102] Additional support for this date comes from Mitchell Dahood as the result of a study of rare parallel word pairs common to Ugaritic and Job.[103] Yet another linguistic study by Avi Hurvitz compares the language of Esther, Ezra, and Chronicles with that of the prose frame-story of Job.[104] He concludes that the latter in its present form seems to require an exilic or post-exilic date, although the content may well be earlier.

VIII. THEOLOGICAL IDEAS

One of the debated issues in the Book of Job is the concept of a mediator. This was a topic touched on in the writer's paper already mentioned.[105] The ideas expressed there owed much to the stimulation of my revered teacher W.A. Irwin. Following Sigmund Mowinckel's earlier article,[106] Irwin had argued that the mysterious figure referred to by Job as מוכיח (9:32-33), עד or שהד (16:19-21) and גאל (19:25-27) was not Yahweh but a third party.[107] He proceeded to trace the subtle development in the function of this shadowy being, pointing out that

---

[102]F.M. Cross, *Canaanite Myth and Hebrew Epic: Essays on the History of the Religion of Israel* (Cambridge, Mass.: Harvard University, 1973) 344, n. 1.

[103]M. Dahood, "Some Rare Parallel Word Pairs in Job and in Ugaritic" (n. 47).

[104]A. Hurvitz, "The Date of the Prose-Tale of Job Linguistically Reconsidered," *Harvard Theological Review* 67 (1974) 17-34.

[105]R.J. Williams, "Theodicy in the Ancient Near East" (n. 1).

[106]S. Mowinckel, "Hiobs *gōʾēl* und Zeuge im Himmel," *Beiträge zur Zeitschrift für die alttestamentliche Wissenschaft* 41 (1925) 207-212.

[107]W.A. Irwin, "An Examination of the Progress of Thought in the Dialogue of Job," *Journal of Religion* 13 (1933) 150-164.

Elihu also alluded to the figure in 33:23-28 as a heavenly מלאך or מליץ.[108]

In the following year Emil Kraeling first drew attention to the striking Ugaritic parallel to Job 19:25.[109]   Advancing beyond these studies, Irwin also commented on the parallels with the Akkadian poem of the Descent of Ishtar in chapter 19,[110] and added that, just as in the Mesopotamian epic the intermediary was a divine messenger, so also this was true of the Ugaritic Myth of Baʿal. Certainty of the course in which Job's own thinking led, however, is impossible, as a result of the damaged state of the third cycle of speeches. Nevertheless, the need for a mediator became paramount in face of the problem of the transcendence of God.

The view that the intermediary was a figure other than Yahweh was also accepted by Robert Pfeiffer,[111] Samuel Terrien,[112] and Friedrich Horst.[113]   Jimmy Roberts, discussing Job 9:27-35 in a brief article, points out that it contains a legal metaphor based on the *rib* and covenant treaty terminology which makes Yahweh both litigant and judge, and consequently demands a third party to the dispute.[114]

---

[108]W.A. Irwin, "The Elihu Speeches in the Criticism of the Book of Job," *Journal of Religion* 17 (1937) 37-47.

[109]E.G. Kraeling, *The Book of the Ways of God* (London: Scribner's Sons, 1938) 89.

[110]W.A. Irwin, "Job's Redeemer," *Journal of Biblical Literature* 81 (1962) 217-229.

[111]R.H. Pfeiffer, *Introduction to the Old Testament* (New York: Harper & Brothers, 1941) 701-702.

[112]S.L. Terrien, "The Book of Job" (n. 12) 1026, 1051-1053; idem, *Job* (n. 14) 133-134, 150-152.

[113]F. Horst, *Hiob* (n. 18) 256.

[114]J.J.M. Roberts, "Job's Summons to Yahweh: The Exploitation of a Legal Metaphor," *Restoration Quarterly* 16 (1973) 159-165.

The claim that Job is portrayed in the Dialogue as a royal figure goes back to Wilhelm Vischer.[115]   A contribution by André Caquot to the Vischer *Festschrift*,[116] draws attention to the royal traits attributed to Job in chapter 29, based on the concept of corporate personality and associated with the New Year festival.   Miloš Bič, basing his remarks on the final form of the Book of Job, also perceives royal characteristics and even messianic traits that depict Job as a Christlike figure.[117]   The poem of Job has been described by Terrien as a "festal tragedy," a royal expiation involving the vicarious suffering of the king and the renewal of the earth through the autumnal rains.[118]   This too is associated with a drama at the New Year festival.

Whether a later addition or an integral part of the original poem, the Yahweh Speeches have usually been thought to have as their aim the evocation of the omnipotence and transcendence of the Deity.   In the opinion of some scholars their effect would then be merely to browbeat the sufferer into abject submission.   The tendency of recent criticism is to understand the significance of the divine confrontation with Job on a much deeper level.

Paul Humbert observed with discernment that the conclusion to be derived is that divine justice does not accord with human ideas of justice.[119]   To demand that God's actions should conform to man's expectations would be a limitation of divine power.   Divine grace is not dependent on man's deserts but on Yahweh's loving favour, and he is not constrained to observe retributive justice.

---

[115]W. Vischer, "Hiob—ein Zeuge Jesu Christi," *Zwischen der Zeiten* 11 (1933) 386-414.

[116]A. Caquot, "Traits royaux dans le personnage de Job," *Maqqēl shâqēdh: la branche d'amandier: Hommage à Wilhelm Vischer* (Montpellier: Causse, Graille, Castelman, 1960) 32-45.

[117]M. Bič, "Le juste et l'impie dans le livre de Job," *Vetus Testamentum Supplements* 15 (1966) 33-43.

[118]S.L. Terrien, "Le poème de Job: drame para-rituel du nouvel-an?" *Vetus Testamentum Supplements* 17 (1969) 220-235.

[119]P. Humbert, "Le modernisme de Job," *Vetus Testamentum Supplements* 3 (1955) 150-161.

Claus Westermann may be called a pioneer of the existentialist approach,[120] which was also adopted by Samuel Terrien in his *Job: Poet of Existence.* There he speaks of a "theology of creative participation."[121] For Georg Fohrer the basis problem of the book is not the theoretical question of theodicy but rather the proper attitude of man in suffering. He finds the answer in Job's final words, a confession of total submission, which he regards as the prerequisite for a spiritual fellowship with the Creator.[122]

John Gray, in a trenchant article,[123] deals with the friends' belief that suffering was both the result and the evidence of sin, the result of which was rejection by and alienation from God. This, he maintains, was upset by the theophany and utterances of the Lord, which revealed the depths of divine grace.

It has frequently been claimed that little or nothing further remains to be said about biblical literature beyond what has already been written. Even this survey, I hope, has shown that studies on the Book of Job are still being produced in great profusion. Indeed, we have by no means as yet succeeded, if we ever shall succeed, in solving all the problems or plumbing all the depths of this profound and enigmatic masterpiece.

---

[120]C. Westermann, *Der Aufbau des Buches Hiob* (Tübingen: J.C.B. Mohr [Paul Siebeck], 1956).

[121]S.L. Terrien, *Job: Poet of Existence* (n. 13) 16.

[122]G. Fohrer, "Das Hiobproblem und seine Lösung," *Wissenschaftliche Zeitschrift der Martin-Luther-Universität Halle* 12 (1963) 249-258; idem, *Das Buch Hiob* (n. 15) 549.

[123]J. Gray, "The Book of Job in the Context of Near Eastern Literature" (n. 29).

JOB AND UGARITIC STUDIES

PETER C. CRAIGIE

The Book of Job has been studied extensively in the context of near eastern literature. Not only the older sources of Sumerian and Akkadian literature, but also the contemporary and later resources of Aramaic and Arabic have been employed in the study of this remarkable book. And almost all new finds of literary texts in the Near East have been drawn into the investigation of Job. It is only a matter of time until studies of Job in the light of the Ebla texts appear, and, if ever we are fortunate enough to find a cache of Edomite texts, no doubt new societies and journals will be established.

But since the discovery of the Ugaritic texts in 1929, and of Akkadian texts from Ras Shamra in subsequent years, Ugaritic Studies have increasingly played an important role in the study of the Book of Job. The potential contributions of Ugaritic studies may be divided into two basic categories: (1) Ugaritic resources have contributed in general to the study of Job, as they have to all other parts of the Hebrew Bible; (2) the discovery of wisdom texts at Ras Shamra has made available a body of more precise data for the examination of the Book of Job in the context of the biblical wisdom tradition.

In the first of these categories, the resources of Ugaritic studies have been applied to the Book of Job as they have to all other biblical books, but the nature of the Book of Job as such has added an element of distinction to this common contribution. The distinctive nature of Job, making it a candidate for more extensive Hebrew-Ugaritic comparative studies than is the case with other biblical books, may be summarized under three points. (1) The book is almost entirely poetic in form; indeed, from a literary perspective, the poetry may be judged to be the best in the ancient Hebrew literary tradition. (2) The language of the book is extremely rich, containing many rare words and forms. (3) The story within the book is not explicitly identified with the Hebrew people or nation.

All these three characteristics of the Book of Job contribute to its appropriateness for Hebrew-Ugaritic studies. (1) The poetic character of the book may be illuminated by the more extensive knowledge of Northwest Semitic poetry that is provided by the study of Ugaritic poetic texts. (2) Likewise, the linguistic and philological problems pertaining to the study of the text of Job may be clarified by the linguistic and philological data made available by a knowledge of Ugaritic language. (3) The search for the provenance of the original story of the Book of Job now has an additional contender to be added to an already long list. In summary, while in principle the general contribution of Ugaritic studies may be the same as that for any other biblical book, in practice the contribution may be greater, given the distinctive character of the book. And this, in turn, creates an awareness of one of the general difficulties pertaining to Job and Ugaritic Studies, namely that not only has Ugaritic shed much light on Job, but also there are more examples of "pan-Ugaritism" in the study of Job than in the study of other biblical books, with the possible exception of the Book of Psalms.

A general example of this tendency can be seen in the writings of Mitchell Dahood and the so-called "Rome School."[1] This tradition in modern scholarship has made a large number of contributions to the study of Job in the light of Ugaritic studies. As in all their contributions, almost every example must be carefully weighed and assessed before being accepted. I will not develop a criticism of the "Rome School" in this context, for it has been done elsewhere.[2] It is,

---

[1]See, for example: M. Dahood, "Some Northwest Semitic Words in Job," *Biblica* 38 (1957) 306-320; idem, "Northwest Semitic Philology and Job," *The Bible in Current Catholic Thought*, ed. J.L. McKenzie (New York: Herder and Herder, 1962) 55-74; idem, "Ḥôl 'Phoenix' in Job 29:18 and in Ugaritic," *The Catholic Biblical Quarterly* 36 (1974) 85-88; idem, "Four Ugaritic Personal Names in Job 39:5, 26-27," *Zeitschrift für die alttestamentliche Wissenschaft* 87 (1975) 220. See further A.C.M. Blommerde, *Northwest Semitic Grammar and Job* (Rome: Biblical Institute Press, 1969).

[2]P.C. Craigie, "Parallel Word Pairs in Ugaritic Poetry," *Ugarit-Forschungen* 11 (1979) 135-140; idem, "Deuteronomy and Ugaritic Studies," *Tyndale Bulletin* 28 (1979) 155-169; idem, "Ugarit and the Bible," *Ugarit in Retrospect*, ed. G. Young (Winona Lake: Eisenbrauns, 1981) 99-111.

however, important to stress that the true worth of this school's contribution to Job studies may not emerge until after a radical assessment both of method and of particular contributions. James Barr has already made a partial critique of aspects of the method,[3] and the critique has been applied in more detail to particular parts of the Book of Job in Lester Grabbe's monograph.[4]

For all my criticism of the "Rome School," it would be folly to underestimate their genuine contributions to a knowledge of the poetry of Job and the rare words and grammatical structures contained in the book. Nor has the literary and philological contribution to Job been limited to the "Rome School." Marvin Pope's commentary in the *Anchor Bible*,[5] and detailed philological studies, such as the recent study of Dennis Pardee,[6] demonstrate clearly the very considerable potential of Ugaritic studies for the clarification of the text and meaning of the Book of Job.

In the larger context, it is the discovery of wisdom texts at Ras Shamra that has made possible a more distinctive study of the Book of Job in the light of data from ancient Ugarit. During the fifteenth, twenty-second, and twenty-fifth campaigns at Ras Shamra, a number of texts were found, in both Sumerian and Akkadian, which indicate clearly the presence of a wisdom tradition in Ugarit. These texts include sayings, a text of the "Counsel" type (analogous to the "Instruction of Šuruppak" or the various Egyptian instructional texts), a part of the Gilgamesh story, and, most significantly, a text concerning

---

[3]J. Barr, *Comparative Philology and the Text of the Old Testament* (Oxford: Clarendon Press, 1968); idem, "Philology and Exegesis. Some General Remarks with Illustrations from Job," *Questions disputées d'Ancien Testament*, ed. C. Brekelmans (Gembloux: Leuven University, 1974) 39-61.

[4]L.L. Grabbe, *Comparative Philology and the Text of Job: A Study in Methodology* (Missoula: Scholars Press, 1977).

[5]M.H. Pope, *Job* (Garden City: Doubleday & Co., Inc., 1965); 3rd rev. ed. (1973).

[6]D. Pardee, "*merôrăt-petanîm* 'venom' in Job 20.14," *Zeitschrift für die alttestamentliche Wissenschaft* 91 (1979) 401-416.

the so-called "Just-Sufferer."[7] The general parallels between these texts and biblical wisdom literature have been examined by Duane Smith and John Khanjian.[8] The "Just Sufferer" text has been examined in some detail by John Gray, in the context of other near eastern wisdom literature.[9] An overall assessment is provided in H.-P. Müller's recent monograph on Job studies.[10]

From the perspective of Job Studies, it is the Akkadian text RS. 25.460, concerning the "Just Sufferer," which has the most immediate relevance. The *terminus ad quem* for the text has been set at c. 1300 B.C., and, in the view of J. Nougayrol, the text may reflect the wisdom tradition of the age of Hammurabi.[11] The text is essentially similar to the so-called "Babylonian Job," or *ludlul bēl nēmeqi*. Thus, from a certain perspective, it does not add much that is radically new, beyond the evidence of the various near eastern texts that were already available for the comparative study of Job. It does, however, bring the comparative evidence closer to the Book of Job, both in time and in place, and at a number of points it may provide closer parallels to the story of Job than does *ludlul bēl nēmeqi*. For example, the sufferer's friends urge him simply to bow to his fate at the hands of the gods, in a fashion similar to the friends of Job. But if one takes the Book of Job as a whole, in its present form, and compares it with this new

---

[7]The principal texts are the following: RS. 15.10 (*Le Palais royal d'Ugarit* 3, 311); RS. 22.219 + 398 (fragment of Gilgamesh); RS. 22.421 (fragment of the Flood Story); RS. 22.439 (*Ugaritica* 5 [1968] 277; a wisdom text of the "counsel" type); RS. 25.130 (*Ugaritica* 5 [1968] 293); RS. 25.424; RS. 25.460 (*Ugaritica* 5 [1968] 268; the "Just Sufferer").

[8]D.E. Smith and J. Khanjian in *Ras Shamra Parallels* 2, ed. L.R. Fisher (Rome: Biblical Institute, 1975) 217-247, 373-400.

[9]J. Gray, "The Book of Job in the Context of Near Eastern Literature," *Zeitschrift für die alttestamentliche Wissenschaft* 82 (1970) 251-269.

[10]H.-P. Müller, *Das Hiobproblem: seine Stellung und Entstehung im alten Orient und im alten Testament* (Darmstadt: Wissenschaftliche Buchgesellschaft, 1978) 56-57.

[11]J. Nougayrol, "Choix de textes littéraires: 162. (Juste) souffrant," *Ugaritica* 5 (1968) 265-273.

wisdom text from Ras Shamra, it is the vast dissimilarities that are far more striking than the similarities.

Hence, if the text RS. 25.460 does have direct relevance to the study of the Book of Job, that relevance is probably to be found in relation to the prehistory of the story on which the Book of Job is based.   Indeed, the tradition of *ludlul bēl nēmeqi*, represented in this Akkadian text from Ras Shamra, may be the source from which the Book of Job developed, as Gray has suggested, though such a proposal must clearly remain hypothetical.   All that is clearly established is that on the Mediterranean coast of Syria, as in Mesopotamia, the issue of the righteous sufferer was known and developed in the context of wisdom literature.   This fact, though slender, adds a link to the chain of the existence of various types of wisdom literature throughout the Ancient Near East.

Though little direct advance in the study of the Book of Job may appear to emerge from the discovery of wisdom texts at Ras Shamra, it is nevertheless possible that in future studies, more definite progress may be made.   Some years ago, Hartmut Gese proposed the existence of a category (or *Gattung*) in Babylonian and Sumerian texts pertaining to the righteous sufferer.[12]   This category, to which *ludlul bēl nēmeqi* belonged, had three parts: (1) a description of the sufferer's plight; (2) the sufferer's lament; (3) a divine response, resulting in the sufferer's healing.   Gese had proposed that the original story, underlying the Book of Job, had belonged to this literary *Gattung*, but that the writer of the extant book had contradicted and changed the religious perspectives implicit in the category in his finished work.   The weakness of the overall hypothesis had been the relative lack of literary data on which it was based; the weakness of the specific hypothesis with respect to Job was the distance, in time and space, that separated the Mesopotamian data from the Book of Job.   To some extent, both these difficulties are reduced by the discovery of RS. 25.460.   The data are increased, and the evidence for the proposed *Gattung* is brought nearer, in time and space, to the context in which the present Book of Job emerged.   But whether or not Gese's thesis can be sustained will depend on further, detailed comparative study of all the data now available.

---

[12]H. Gese, *Lehre und Wirklichkeit in der alten Weisheit: Studien zu den Sprüchen Salomos und zu dem Buche Hiob* (Tübingen: J.C.B. Mohr, 1958) 51-78.

Until the present, the comparative study of the Book of Job and wisdom literature from Ras Shamra has worked on the general assumption that there has not survived any wisdom literature in the Ugaritic language as such. Nevertheless, it is possible that a review of the currently known Ugaritic literary texts may necessitate a revision of the view that they contain no wisdom literature.[13] More precisely, it is possible, though by no means certain, that the so-called "Legend of AQHAT" may be classified as a wisdom text. The general difficulty of making firm classifications of the Ugaritic literary texts is further exacerbated in this case by the incompleteness of the text.

The "Legend of AQHAT" is preserved on three clay tablets; the second, in the sequence of the story, is badly mutilated, and the third tablet is broken in such a fashion that the climax and conclusion of the story remains unknown. (All three tablets were discovered in 1930 in the High Priest's library; the passage of time since that initial discovery is such that the missing fragment is unlikely to be found.) The conclusion of the story may be critical to its interpretation and classification. If Pughat, in her attempt to avenge her brother's death, also died in the attempt, that final sad event would tint the story as a whole. The story of the patriarchal figure of Daniel would be essentially one of grief, in the loss first of a son, then of a daughter, at the hands of apparently capricious deities.

If the "Legend of AQHAT" were to be classified as a kind of wisdom text, it would not of course make it any more or less similar to the Book of Job. Nevertheless, there are similarities. Both the Legend and the Book of Job are fine literary works, yet neither reflect the culture in which they are found. The "Legend of AQHAT" appears to reflect a period more ancient and less urban than that of the kingdom of Ugarit, as does the Book of Job in the context of Hebrew society. And both Job and Daniel are patriarchal figures, whose grief comes in part from the death of children.

But it would be folly to press the similarities between the two texts too far. What is more probable is that both texts, in addition to

---

[13]H.P. Dressler, in a paper presented to the Pacific Northwest Region of the Society of Biblical Literature, May 8, 1981, proposed the possibility that *AQHAT* may be viewed as a wisdom text; the view will be presented in more detail in a forthcoming monograph on the *AQHAT* text.

the Babylonian story of Gilgamesh, belong to a general literary tradition in the wisdom schools, in which the fundamental problems of human existence are examined in a religious and literary perspective. The Epic of Gilgamesh was certainly well known, both at Ugarit and in the geographical region of Palestine.[14] Perhaps the story of Job and the story of AQHAT (or, more precisely, the story of Daniel) were similar popular traditions, widely known throughout the Ancient Near East. Indeed, the linking of Noah, Daniel, and Job (Ezekiel 14:4 and 20) may be an allusion to the three ancient literary works in which these three figures (or their equivalents) are mentioned, namely the Epic of Gilgamesh (with its account of the flood), the Legend of AQHAT/Daniel, and the Book of Job. All three figures are in some sense the archetypes of ancient wisdom, around which the stories of the wisdom literature have crystallized. And all three texts, which may be classified loosely under the label of wisdom, somehow transcend the immediate environment in which they have survived; their universal appeal and fascination are rooted in their focus on one of the most fundamental problems of human existence.

In conclusion, what is the current status of the Book of Job in the context of Ugaritic studies? A great deal has been done, but much more remains to be done. What remains to be done can be summarized in three parts. (1) There remains a massive task of assessing and reviewing the earlier comparative studies, of a literary and philological nature, particularly those of the "Rome School." In my own experience of undertaking this task of assessment in another context (the study of the Psalms), more than fifty percent of former proposals may be rejected, but what remains represents significant progress in the understanding of the text, grammar, and literary form of the book. (2) Further comparative work of a literary and philological nature remains to be done. The extant Ugaritic resources are becoming increasingly better known and supplemented by new finds, both at Ras Shamra and Ras Ibn Hani. These refined data and new data will make possible further progress in comparative studies of all kinds. (3) Finally, more remains to be done in the particular study of

---

[14]A thirteenth century fragment of the Epic was found at Megiddo. See A. Goetze and S. Levy, "A Fragment of the Gilgamesh Epic from Megiddo," *Atiqot* 2 (1959) 121-128. On the fragment from Ugarit, see footnote 7 (above).

Job in the context of wisdom literature from Ras Shamra. Not only the text entitled the "Just Sufferer," but also the "Legend of AQHAT" offer real promise for further illumination of the Book of Job.

ELIHU'S SECOND SPEECH
ACCORDING TO
THE SEPTUAGINT

CLAUDE E. COX

INTRODUCTION

The Septuagint (LXX) translation of Job varies considerably from the received Hebrew text (MT). The most noticeable difference is that the LXX text is about one-sixth shorter. Much of the attention that the Greek Job has received has centered on the question: "Why is the LXX text shorter?" To this question five responses have been given.

(1) LXX Job is shorter than the MT because its Hebrew parent text was shorter. For Edwin Hatch this meant that the MT is an expansion of that shorter original.[1] Recently, Harry Orlinsky has revived this view, though he does not argue that the MT is an expansion. Rather, the Hebrew text of Job was extant in two forms when the translation into Greek was made, and the LXX rests on the shorter one. He is able to appeal to the case of LXX Jeremiah which is one-eighth shorter than the MT: the Dead Sea Scrolls have shown that LXX Jeremiah is based on a shorter Hebrew original.[2] Hatch's view did not gain any acceptance; it is yet to be seen whether Orlinsky will be able to offer compelling reasons for his assertion.

---

[1]E. Hatch, *Essays in Biblical Greek* (Oxford: The Clarendon Press, 1889) 214, cited in H.B. Swete, *An Introduction to the Old Testament in Greek*, rev. R.R. Ottley (Cambridge: University Press, 1914); reprinted (New York: KTAV, 1968) 256.

[2]H.M. Orlinsky, "The Hebrew *Vorlage* of the Septuagint of the Book of Joshua," *Vetus Testamentum Supplements* 17 (1968) 194.

The other four responses are of a different kind in that the responsibility for the shorter text of LXX Job is placed with the translator.

(2) At times the shorter LXX text may be the result of parablepsis by homoioteleuton: the scribe's eye skipped from one word to a later one ending in the same letters.[3] This would mean that the translator was sometimes careless.[4] This carelessness, if it exists, cannot account for the majority of the cases in which the LXX is shorter than the MT.

(3) Donald Gard, in a thesis supervised by Henry Gehman, argued that theological reasons are responsible for the shorter text.[5] That the translator had a theological perspective is not surprising; at times it is reflected in his translation. For example, the translator may stress the transcendence of God: at 13:3 Job says, "I would speak to the Almighty" (*RSV*) to which the LXX adds "if he wills it." That elsewhere the text was shortened for the same reason or, for example, to avoid anthropomorphism, is quite likely. However, that which seeks to prove too much proves little, and Gard's argument cripples itself because it claims too much and because it is based upon examples that are too subjectively assessed and often unconvincing.[6]

(4) Another response to the question, "Why is the LXX shorter?" is that the translator did not understand some passages in the Hebrew text because they are so difficult: these he abbreviated or omitted. See, for example, Dhorme's comment at 37:12, "The tendency of G is

---

[3]See for example, the comments on Job 34:3ff. and 35:3,14, in E.P. Dhorme, *Le livre de Job* (Paris: Victor Lecoffre, 1926); Eng. trans., *A Commentary on the Book of Job* (London: Nelson, 1967).

[4]See Dhorme's comments on Job 35:13, ibid.

[5]D.H. Gard, *The Exegetical Method of the Greek Translator of the Book of Job* (Philadelphia: Society of Biblical Literature, 1952); reprinted (1967).

[6]In 1954, J.W. Wevers was willing to acknowledge that theological outlook was one of the participating factors which resulted in the shorter text. See his remarks about Gard's study in "Septuaginta - Forschungen," *Teologische Rundschau* 22 (1954) 188.

to shorten in these difficult passages."[7] Recently, Jonas Greenfield has offered a similar evaluation: "The early translator into Greek no longer understood many passages and so omitted them . . . ."[8] Some of the differences between the MT and LXX Job are indeed attributable to difficulties inherent in the Hebrew text: it was unpointed, permitting the same word to be read in more than one way; continuous script posed the problem of the proper division of words within a verse and raised the issue of where words or phrases belonged, with what preceded or with what followed; letters paleographically similar led to their easy confusion, especially *daleth* and *resh*, *waw* and *yod*, *hē* and *ḥēth*; Job contains many words that are *hapax legomena* or are very rare; the Hebrew text is at times corrupt or incomprehensible. It should also be mentioned that Job is one of the *Kethubim* ("Writings"), and a scribe might not be as familiar with its text and content as with the Law or Prophets, nor, probably, regard it as of quite the same importance.

The question about how many of the shorter passages might be attributed to the factor of difficulty remains. Certainly not all, since the translator does translate some difficult passages while passing over others that are quite simple. There seems to be a certain arbitrariness on the part of the translator. It would appear that level of difficulty is not the only factor to be considered.

(5) Finally, Dhorme says that the translator omitted passages which seemed to have no use (*inutile*) and abbreviated those which were too long.[9] A similar but more extensive argumentation is given by G. Gerleman, who says that the translator sought to restrict the repetition of ideas in the Hebrew text by shortening it. This applies to individual verses, to long sections, and to poetic digressions that seem to depart from the theme of the book. The translator sometimes omits

---

[7]E.P. Dhorme, *Le Livre de Job* (n. 3) 515. Dhorme (p. 497) notes that Ehrlich refused to translate 36:16-19 because this passage seemed incomprehensible.

[8]J.C. Greenfield, *The Book of Job* (Philadelphia: The Jewish Publication Society of America, 1980) xiv.

[9]E.P. Dhorme, *Le livre de Job* (n. 3) clxii.

and often offers a résumé of a passage.[10] It is true that Job in the MT is repetitious; the arguments end essentially with chapter 23. Credibility is lent to this line of argument by Dhorme's observation concerning LXX Job as a whole: the difference in length between the MT and the LXX increases from the beginning of the Prologue to the Epilogue: the LXX is four percent shorter to chapter 15; sixteen percent in 15-21; twenty-five percent in 22-31; thirty-five percent in 32-37; and sixteen percent in the Epilogue, 38-42.[11] However, it must be pointed out that the LXX text is occasionally longer than the MT, so it would appear that the translator was not simply seeking the shortest possible text.

Each of these five responses has something to commend it. If previous studies are to be faulted it is because they have tended to be atomistic and/or to make one response the solution to the whole problem. The question of the shorter text must be pursued as part of an attempt to understand its nature as a translation. For example, it has often been commented that the LXX paraphrases the Hebrew. Does this observation not influence our view of the translator's attitude toward his Hebrew text? Would this attitude have led him to abbreviate? Perhaps, but the probability of the correctness of such a conclusion rests upon one's view of the nature of the shorter text generally. For this reason the interest of this paper is less with the "why?" and "how?" than with "what is the result?" of the shortness of LXX Job. For pursuing the question "what is the result?" the Elihu speeches were chosen, a section of text of restricted size in which the LXX is thirty-five percent shorter than the MT. Even this section is too extensive to be dealt with briefly. Therefore Elihu's second speech (chapter 34) has been selected: it has a clear structure and is ten and one-half verses shorter in the LXX.[12]

Elihu's second speech is a wisdom speech beginning with an introduction (1-9) in which Elihu invites "the wise" to listen and in

---

[10]G. Gerleman, *Studies in the Septuagint: I. Book of Job* (Lund: C.W.K. Gleerup, 1946) 22-25.

[11]E.P. Dhorme, *Le livre de Job* (n. 3) clxii.

[12]The Greek text used is Alfred Rahlfs' provisional text of 1935, *Septuaginta* (Stuttgart: Württembergische Bibelanstalt, 1965).

which he cites Job's claims. Elihu then contests Job's thesis (10-11). This is followed by an extensive substantiation of Elihu's argument (12-33). Finally, there is a conclusion in which Job's views are condemned (34-37).[13] Each of the four sections of the chapter is shorter than MT except the conclusion. In what way is the LXX text shorter and what effect does this have upon the progression of thought?

I.

In the introduction Elihu invites the wise to listen to him (1-2). He employs a simile (they should test words like the palate tests food [3]), and asks them to render a judgment concerning Job's ideas (4). Elihu then quotes several of Job's claims (5-6) beginning with "I am innocent." Next, Job's views are assumed to be damnable (7-9): first he is likened to someone who drinks scoffing like water (7); then he is accused of keeping bad company (8); and further, as if to score one more point, Elihu quotes one more Joban thesis to the effect that serving God has no value (9).

The LXX lacks vv. 3, 4, 6b, and 7. That the Greek goes from v. 2 to v. 5 means that Elihu's exhortation to his wise friends to determine what is right (4) "because Job has said" such and such (5) is lost. Instead, the wise are asked to hear Elihu (2) "because Job has said [5]." The loss of vv. 3-4 may be the result of a simple error. "What is good" at the end of v. 4 in the MT appears at the end of v. 2 in the LXX (so, "Give attention to what is good"). This gives some weight to Dhorme's suggestion that vv. 3-4 have been lost by parablepsis through homoioteleuton, האזנו (2) to בירנו (4).[14] The loss of these verses would then be the result of a simple, careless mistake. However, like v. 7, v. 3 contains a simile. Since the simile of v. 7 does not appear in the LXX it must be asked whether the lack of v. 3 in the LXX is deliberate. If so, then v. 4 is also deliberately omitted, and the attachment of the end of v. 4 to v. 2 is a bridge which the translator found convenient.

---

[13]An outline of Job 34 may be found on pages 50-53 (below). The basic structural arrangement is from C. Westermann, *Der Aufbau des Buches Job* (Tübingen: J.C.B. Mohr [Paul Siebeck], 1956) 112ff.

[14]E.P. Dhorme, *Le livre de Job* (n. 3) 464.

In vv. 5-6 Elihu cites a number of the charges that Job has made. The charge in v. 6 is: "in spite of my right I am counted a liar [6a]; my wound in incurable, though I am without transgression [6b]." The LXX appears not to have vv. 6b or 7. However, a glance at LXX v. 8 will show that the last half of v. 6b has been added to the beginning of v. 8.[15] Further, the meaning of v. 8 has been turned about: in the Hebrew, Elihu accuses Job of keeping bad company, while in the LXX, the translator continues the Joban complaint of v. 6, namely "but he falsified my judgment [6a], [omit 7], not being a sinner nor impious [LXX 8a = MT 6bβ], nor having shared the way of the doers of iniquity [LXX 8b = MT 8a], in order to go with the impious [LXX 8c = MT 8b]." So the sense of v. 8 is exactly reversed, and the fact that v. 8 is part of a question in the Hebrew is lost because the LXX does not have v. 7. The LXX lacks v. 6bα, possibly for a theological motive: God can heal all wounds! More noteworthy is the way in which MT v. 6bβ has been used as a bridge to v. 8 and the changes this has brought about there.

It is not clear why the LXX lacks v. 7. As noted, it is a simile. Did the translator think it unnecessary or an interruption in the train of thought?

II.

The second section of chapter 34 is contained in vv. 10-11. Here Elihu contests Job's thesis that God has acted unjustly. Once again Elihu solicits attention (10a). He asserts that God does not do wickedness (10b) or wrong (10c). Rather, God deals with a person according to that person's work (11a) and ways (11b). Both verses contain synonymous parallelism.

The LXX lacks v. 11b. It translates v. 11 "but he returns to man just as each one of them does," a quite adequate rendering of the thought of the verse. The same thing might well have been done with v. 10. There is no apparent reason for the shorter text at v. 11; it seems quite arbitrary.

We may also note that the Greek of v. 10bc differs considerably from the MT. In the LXX the defense is not now of God but of the

---

[15]Ibid., 466.

speaker, Elihu: "May it not be mine to act impiously before the Lord and before the Almighty to throw what is righteous into confusion." The Greek has points of contact with the Hebrew but otherwise seems to go its own way.

Elihu's contest of Job's ideas, vv. 10-11, is not only slightly shorter but quite different in the LXX.

III.

The third and longest section of chapter 34 is vv. 12-33.   Here Elihu substantiates his contention that God does no wrong.   In general, Elihu tells his hearers that God is powerful and impartial, and he explains at length how God punishes the wicked.   This punishment, Elihu says, is intended to chastise them.   In this third section, the LXX is almost one-third shorter than the MT, lacking vv. 18b, 23a, 25b, and 28-33.

Elihu begins by restating the contention (12) made in v. 10.   The LXX preserves v. 12, but alters the beginning of the verse from "surely" followed by a statement in the negative to a rhetorical question expecting a negative answer: "Do you think that the Lord will do wrong?"   Elihu then asserts that there is no one above God (13) and that all life is dependent upon God (14-15).   The LXX paraphrases v. 13, "Who made the earth and who is the one who makes what is under heaven and all existing things?"

In v. 16 Elihu once again begs for attention.   This verse seems somewhat intrusive, and Westermann takes it to be the title for the fourth speech in chapter 36.   He also removes vv. 14-15.[16]   The Greek is not shorter.

In vv. 17-20 Elihu stresses God's power and impartiality.   Elihu says it is inconceivable that the ruler of the world should be unjust (17) and goes on to offer proof of God's power and impartiality: he asserts himself over kings (18a) and nobles (18b); he treats all princes alike (19a) and is evenhanded with rich and poor (19b) because he has made them all (19c).   Finally, he can take human life away in death (20).   The LXX lacks v. 18b which in the MT reads "[who says] to nobles 'Wicked man'."   The loss of this half line of the Hebrew has no

---

[16]C. Westermann, *Der Aufbau des Buches Job* (n. 12) 112.

effect upon the argument Elihu is making. Why not translate it? It is possible that the translator read the adjective רשע as its cognate verb "do wickedly." This possibility gains likelihood when one notices that the verse has a chiastic structure, רשע standing in a position parallel to "he who says." The translator would have wished to avert any notion that God acts wrongly and so omitted v. 18b. However, it will also be noted that v. 18b makes no sense after the Greek of v. 18a. The Greek turns the sense of v. 18a completely about: it is not now God speaking to a king and saying "worthless one," but a man speaking to a king (so God?). Further, the Greek reads the last word of v. 17 with v. 18 and introduces the law: the Greek says, "[It's an] impious [man] who says to a king, 'You are breaking the law'." It might then be argued that the loss of v. 18b came about not because of a theological concern but because v. 18b did not make sense after the LXX translation of 18a.

On a line-for-line basis, there would appear to be no further omissions in LXX vv. 17-20. However, a look at v. 19 indicates that the Greek has not rendered v. 19c ("for they are all the work of his hands") but replaced it with a line that is parallel to v. 19a. The Greek of v. 19 reads "Who did not stop before the honoured, nor know enough to give honour to princes, to admire their faces." The Greek of vv. 17-19 becomes a rewrite of the Hebrew. In the Hebrew these verses refer to God's power over men and the necessity of honouring him. In the Greek they are a castigation of Job for not considering God and being impious, for not recognizing one greater than himself.

If LXX vv. 17-19 differs from the MT, this is no less true of v. 20. Orlinsky does not deal with it in connection with his discussion of ἀδύνατος (which occurs in the last line) because the LXX differs too radically from the MT.[17] Dhorme says that it is impossible to harmonize the Greek and Hebrew but suggests that we may be dealing with a paraphrase.[18] The point of the Greek seems to be that if we rightly honour the great (18-19) whose honour is a thing of no lasting duration (20) how much more ought we to honour God?

---

[17]H. Orlinsky, "Studies in the Septuagint of the Book of Job," *Hebrew Union College Annual* 35 (1964) 74.

[18]E.P. Dhorme, *Le livre de Job* (n. 3) 472.

More than half of the third section of Elihu's speech in chapter 34 is devoted to his assertion that God sees all men's deeds and that he punishes the wicked (21-33). The emphasis is upon the latter (24-33). The Greek lacks vv. 23a, 25b, and 28-33.

First, Elihu claims that God sees everything that a man does (21); therefore evildoers have no place to hide (22). The Greek of these verses offers a paraphrase of the Hebrew but accurately conveys the sense of the original. For example, the Hebrew "There is no gloom or deep darkness where evildoers may hide themselves" becomes "Nor will there be a place that the doers of lawlessness may hide."

Second, in v. 23, Elihu seems to be saying that God can summon a man before him at any time. The *RSV* reads "For he has not appointed a time for any man to go before God in judgment." The LXX has nothing for v. 23a; nor does it translate v. 23b. What stands as v. 23b is a summary of v. 21 "for the Lord observes all people" which follows nicely upon v. 22. This means that the translator left the entirety of v. 23 untranslated but at the same time felt free to emphasize again the notion of v. 21. Rather than avoiding repetition he has created it. The meaning of v. 23 is puzzling, and it seems probable that the translator noticed this as well as the fact that the transition from vv. 22 to 24 is an easy one. The sequence of thought is preserved.

Third, Elihu points out how God shatters the wicked without notice (24) either in the night (25) or in public (26), and the reasons are given for this (27-30). Fourth, Elihu argues that the punishment of the wicked is for their chastisement (31-33).

The LXX treatment of v. 24 is noteworthy. In the first half of the verse the translator has read ירע "shatter," as ירע "know" (confusion of *daleth* and *resh*), so that instead of "He shatters the mighty without investigation" the LXX reads "He is the one who understands unsearchable things." "Unsearchable things" has apparently reminded the translator of v. 9:10 of which he now gives us the second half instead of translating the second half of v. 24.[19] So instead of "and sets others in their place" we have "splendid and extraordinary things of which there is no number." This means that v. 24 in the Greek carries on the thought of vv. 21-22, God's omniscience. The translator's practice of quoting another text rather than translating the one before him is not unique to this verse in chapter 34.

---

[19]Ibid., 475.

The idea of God's knowing men's deeds is continued in v. 25a, so also in the LXX. However, the LXX lacks v. 25b which says "he overturns them in the night, and they are crushed." Gard suggested that there is a theological reason for the shorter text: the Greek omits v. 25b because it seems to depict the omnipotence of God only with reference to destruction.[20] This is not convincing, especially since in the very next half-verse the Greek has God extinguishing the impious. It is possible that the repetition of the same idea twice in succession led the translator to abbreviate by omitting v. 25b. This line of argument is hazardous too, since there are so many similar instances in which the Greek follows the Hebrew.

In v. 26 God strikes down the wicked publicly: "He strikes them for their wickedness in the sight of men" (RSV). The Greek reads for the first part "He extinguished the impious; they were visible before him" (reading with Rahlfs).

In vv. 27-30 the reasons for God's actions against the wicked are listed: they turned away from him (27); the cry of the afflicted came to him (28); he does not want the godless to rule (30).[21] Of these verses, and therefore reasons, the LXX has only v. 27. This means that Elihu's entire explanation for the destruction of the wicked is now sustained by v. 27, which therefore deserves careful attention.

LXX v. 27 is significant not only because it is now the complete explication for the destruction of the wicked but also because of the way the translator has chosen to interpret the Hebrew. The Hebrew says that the wicked are destroyed "because they turned aside from following him [27a] and had no regard for any of his ways [27b]." For v. 27a, the LXX says "because they turned aside from the law of God." For the translator, to turn aside from following God means to turn aside from the law. In v. 27b, the LXX reads "and his requirements [δικαιώματα] they did not know." The translation of דרך by δικαίωμα "commandment," or "requirement," occurs only here in the LXX. δικαίωμα is parallel to "the law" in v. 27 and means much the same thing.

---

[20]D.H. Gard, *The Exegetical Method of the Greek Translator of the Book of Job* (n. 5) 66.

[21]Verse 29 is a parenthetical remark.

In vv. 31-33 Elihu advances his argument that God punishes the wicked to chastise them. In vv. 31-32 Elihu seems to offer a conjectural confession, a model for Job; in v. 33 Elihu challenges Job to accept God's chastisement.

The LXX lacks vv. 28-30 (reasons for the destruction of the wicked) and vv. 31-33 (evildoers are punished to chastise them). Why? The *RSV* in a footnote says "The Hebrew of verses 29-33 is obscure." This is certainly true. Verse 24 is some sort of parenthetical remark to the effect that God reveals himself only when he wishes (?). The intent of Elihu's conjectural confession in vv. 31-32 is not clear. And what does "declare what you know [33b]" mean? The Hebrew is certainly difficult. Is this a reason why a translator would omit it? Perhaps, yet there are other difficult passages which the translator has tried to translate, at least in part (cf. 36:16-19).

Aside from the difficulty of the Hebrew, there is another reason why the translator might have omitted vv. 31-33. Elihu's argument that God punishes human beings to chastise them has already been presented at some length in chapter 33 (see vv. 14-33 [of which the LXX lacks vv. 19b, 20b, 28, 29, 31b, 32-33]). Given the difficulty of the Hebrew, the translator may have decided that Elihu's argument need not be given again. The reason for the shorter Greek text is therefore twofold. This accounts for vv. 29-33. Verse 28 was also omitted because it added nothing to the all-encompassing charge of v. 27.

That the LXX lacks vv. 28-33 means that the entire explanation for the punishment of the wicked rests on v. 27. In the Hebrew of vv. 24-26, God shatters (24), destroys (25) and strikes down (26) the wicked. By omission of v. 25b and interpretation in vv. 24 and 26, the LXX emphasizes God's all-knowingness. Verses 24-26 lead up to v. 27: for the LXX this all-knowingness refers to God's ability to see man's breaking of the Law. Elihu in the Greek is arguing that Job is suffering because of his wickedness, i.e., a turning from the Law. God, who perceives all things, has seen his transgression.

IV.

The conclusion to Elihu's speech is contained in 34:34-37. Elihu begins by stating that the wise who have heard his argument (34) will surely draw the conclusion "Job speaks without knowledge, his words are without insight [35]." Elihu establishes here a consensus opinion: all the wise stand against Job. This consensus permits Elihu to call for the continued chastisement of Job, to the death (36a). This should be done because Job's ideas are those of the wicked (36b). The "without knowledge" of v. 35 is clarified in v. 36b: the knowledge that Job lacks and refuses to recognize is that of the wise, a revealed knowledge. Finally, in v. 37 Elihu adds more damning charges against Job: Job has refused to recognize God's discipline (37a), disclaims those who have true insight (37b), and makes much talk against God (37c). Thus, Elihu's speech ends with a strong and comprehensive condemnation with which all of the wise are expected to agree.

The Greek text of vv. 34-37 is not shorter than the Hebrew. However, the Greek is considerably different from the Hebrew. In vv. 34 and 35, both of which contain the repetition of synonymous parallelism, there is little difference. In v. 34a, "will say to me" becomes "will say these things," and v. 34b, "who hears me," becomes "[who] listened to what I said." In each case the emphasis is shifted from Elihu to his argument; but this is a minor difference.

In vv. 36 and 37 the Greek is quite different from the Hebrew, to the extent that Job, Elihu, and Elihu's speech are put in a different light. Verses 36 and 37 read in the LXX, "But nevertheless, learn, O Job,/ May you not offer again an answer like the foolish,/ Lest we should add to our sins/ and lawlessness be reckoned to us/ while saying many things before the Lord." There is no mention of any further chastisement of Job here: the Greek seems to read בין "learn," for יבחן "test," "try."[22] The LXX also adds "again" to v. 36: thus, Job is asked to learn his lesson and not to repeat the mistake of arguing contrary to wisdom. In v. 37 the Greek means something quite different from the Hebrew: in the Hebrew the condemnation of Job continues, but in the Greek it is Job, Elihu, the friends, and the wise who are to be worried lest they together add to their sins. One suspects that neither Job, nor Elihu, nor the other friends would have been happy with this resolution of the argument. The charge that concerns the Greek Elihu is "lawlessness" (ἀνομία) which takes us back to v. 27, wherein lies for the LXX the basis of the charge against Job: Job departed from the Law. Now the charge that Job has raised puts them all, by its very argumentation, in danger of a charge of disregard

---

[22]E.P. Dhorme, *Le livre de Job* (n. 3) 481.

for the Law, the proper understanding of which, it seems, belongs to "the wise." The reader's perspective on Job's fate at the end of chapter 34 in the Greek is quite different from that of the Hebrew. The Hebrew text leaves one expecting Job to die being disciplined; the Greek text leaves one anticipating some other conclusion yet to come.

                                      V.

What then, is the nature of the shorter text of Greek Job? In Elihu's second speech the meaning of the Hebrew is completely changed several times (8, 10, 18, 20, 36-37); on another occasion the translator offers a crucial interpretation of the Joban dilemma (27); several times the Hebrew has been paraphrased (13, 20, 22); three times the translator replaces a part of a verse, twice with a thought from the near context (19c from 19a; 23b from 21), once from a distant text (24b from 9:10). Throughout these changes the translator seems to be governed by a conception of what the book of Job means for his own day (cf. v. 27). The application of this conception results in a translation that can hardly be termed literal: it is free but at the same time rather arbitrary in places.

This summary of the nature of the translated parts of chapter 34 makes it highly probable that the shorter LXX text is to be attributed to abbreviation by the translator. No single factor accounts for all the instances of shortening in chapter 34: the longest section, vv. 28-33, seems to have been left out because of the difficulty of the Hebrew and to curtail repetition; v. 23 may have been left out because its meaning is unclear; v. 6bα may have been passed over for theological reasons; v. 18b was not translated because it made no sense after LXX v. 18a (i.e., the omission is contextually based); the omission of v. 7 may be contextual since the simile could have no place within the translator's rendering of vv. 6b and 8; several times (3ff. [unless by mistake], 11b, 25b) the omissions seem quite arbitrary and without specific intent, unless simply to shorten the text. The arbitrary nature of the translator's work is seen when one asks why he abbreviated where he did: why did he not, for example, leave out v. 16?

It is to be noted that the LXX text has been shortened with a sensitivity for continuity: the translator has skillfully bridged the thought from vv. 2 to 5; 6bβ to 8; 22 to 24; 27 to 34. This too is an indication that the LXX translation of Job is a work of artistic deliberation.

ELIHU'S SECOND SPEECH (CHAPTER 34)

I. Introduction (34:1-9)   LXX lacks

   A. Invitation to "the wise" to
      listen

      1. Elihu identified as
         speaker   1
      2. The wise addressed   2
      3. Elihu uses a simile:
         ears test words like
         the palate tests food   3   3

   B. Elihu asks his hearers to
      resolve to find a judgment
      concerning Job   4   4
   C. Job's theses are quoted

      1. "I am innocent"   5a
      2. "God has taken away
         my right"   5b
      3. "In spite of my right
         I am counted a liar"   6a
      4. "My wound is incurable
         though I am without
         transgression"   6b   6b

   D. The condemnation of Job's
      views assumed

      1. Job is likened to someone
         who drinks scoffing like
         water   7   7
      2. Job is accused of keeping
         company with

         a. Evildoers   8a
         b. Wicked men   8b

      3. Another thesis of Job is
         regarded as grounds of
         condemnation: "It is of
         no profit to take delight
         in God"   9

II. Job's thesis is contested (34:10-11)

    A. Elihu asks his hearers   10a
    B. God does not do

        1. Wickedness or   10b
        2. Wrong   10c

    C. God rewards a man
       according to

        1. "The work of a man"   11a
        2. "His ways"   11b   11b

III. Elihu substantiates his contention
    (34:12-33)

    A. Elihu restates the
       contention of v. 10b,c   12
    B. There is no one above God 13
    C. All life is dependent upon
       God   14-15
    D. Elihu asks his hearers to
       listen   16
    E. God's power and
       impartiality are stressed

        1. It is inconceivable that
           the one who governs the
           world should hate justice 17a
        2. How can Job condemn the
           one who is right and
           mighty   17b
        3. Proof of God's power
           and impartiality

           a. He can call a king
              "worthless one"   18a
           b. He can say to a
              noble "wicked man" 18b   18b
           c. He is not partial
              to one prince over
              another   19a
           d. He has no more
              regard for rich than
              poor   19b
           e. The reason is given
              for God's impartiality:
              He made all human
              beings   19c   cf.19a

f. He can take human
   life away in death   20

F. God sees all man's deeds;
   he punishes the wicked

  1. He sees everything that
     a man does   21
  2. Evildoers have no place
     to hide   22
  3. He can summon a man
     before him at any time   23   23a cf.b
  4. God's treatment of the
     wicked

    a. He shatters the
       wicked without notice
       and puts others in
       their place   24
    b. He overturns them
       in the night   25   25b
    c. Or, he strikes them
       down in public   26
    d. Reasons for God's
       actions against the
       wicked are given

       1) They turned away
          from him   27
       2) The cry of those
          whom the wicked
          afflicted came to
          him   28   28
       3) A parenthetical
          remark is made:
          God reveals himself
          only when he
          wishes   29   29
       4) He does not want
          the godless to
          reign   30   30

  5. Evildoers are punished to
     chastise them

    a. Elihu offers a
       conjectural confession

1) The evildoer recognizes his chastisement and says he will not offend God any more	31	31
2) The evildoer seeks God's guidance and says he will sin no more	32	32

b. Elihu challenges Job to accept chastisement

1) God will not change Job's lot until Job accepts the chastisement	33a	33a
2) The choice is Job's	33b	33b

IV. Conclusion: Job's views are condemned (34:34-37)

A. Elihu solicits the agreement of his audience	34
B. Judgment is rendered against Job's views	35
C. Job's claims are said to be groundless	35a
D. Elihu asks for further chastisement of Job	36
E. The reasons for Elihu's appeal are listed	

1. Job's answers are like those of the wicked	36b
2. Job adds rebellion to his sin	37a
3. Job rejects the advice of the wise	37b
4. Job multiplies his words against God	37c

ARAMAIC STUDIES
AND THE BOOK OF JOB

WALTER E. AUFRECHT

INTRODUCTION

Until recently, the study of Aramaic language and literature has been a sideline pursued by those who are otherwise engaged in related fields. In the last two decades, however, it has become a major discipline in its own right, pursued by a world-wide community of scholars.[1]

The reason for this is that Aramaic language and literature provides controls for a large number of disciplines: Semitic philology and paleography, Northwest Semitic epigraphy, biblical textual studies and exegesis, and historical studies of several kinds, not the least of which include the history of Judaism and Christianity. Indeed, it is the field of religious studies that today most benefits from the study of Aramaic language and literature.

The student of Judaism must know Aramaic not only because portions of the Hebrew Bible are written in Aramaic and because the Talmud is written in Aramaic, but because the Targums Onkelos and Jonathan are official translations of scripture. As the Talmud says, the weekly portion is to be read privately "twice in the original and once in the Targum" (*b. Ber.* 8a). In addition to these, many documents

---

[1]See *Newsletter for Targumic and Cognate Studies*, ed. E.G. Clarke (Dept. of Near Eastern Studies: University of Toronto, Toronto, Ontario. M5S 1A1.).

written in Aramaic—both devotional and non-devotional—illuminate the
history, beliefs, and practices of the Jewish people.[2]

Because Christianity originated in an Aramaic-speaking milieu,[3]
the student of early Christianity wishing to know something of the
Semitic background of the New Testament must be familiar with
biblical, Palestinian, and Galilean Aramaic.[4] The historian of the early
church must know something of Syriac and its literature, because it was
in this Aramaic dialect that much of Christian theology was first
expressed.[5]

In passing, it should be noted that the historian of matters secular
cannot afford to ignore any of these, nor the material in the Aramaic
dialects of Nabatean, Palmyrean, and Mandaic; nor the Aramaic
contribution to Greek, Assyrian, Persian and Arabic languages and
literatures.[6]

In short, the literature in Aramaic is vast, from the earliest
inscriptions dated c. 1000 B.C., to the literature of the modern
communities of Maʿlula (Western Aramaic) and Kurdistan (Eastern

---

[2]For a survey of Aramaic with special reference to those dialects used
by Jews, see J.C. Greenfield, "Aramaic and its Dialects," *Jewish
Languages, Theme and Variations*, ed. H.H. Paper (Cambridge, Mass.:
Association for Jewish Studies, 1978) 29-43.

[3]M. McNamara, "The Spoken Aramaic of First Century Palestine,"
Church Ministry, ed. A. Mayes (Dublin: Dominican Publications, 1977)
95-138.

[4]On these dialects and the development of Aramaic, see:
F. Rosenthal, *Die Aramaistische Forschung* (Leiden: E. J. Brill, 1964);
E.Y. Kutscher, "Aramaic," *Current Trends in Linguistics* 6, ed. T.A.
Sebeok (The Hague: Mouton, 1970) 347-412; idem, "Aramaic,"
Encyclopaedia judaica 1 (Jerusalem: The Macmillan Co., 1971) 259-287;
J.A. Fitzmyer, "The Phases of the Aramaic Language," *A Wandering
Aramean, Collected Aramaic Essays* (Missoula: Scholars Press, 1979)
57-83.

[5]W.S. McCullough, *A Short History of Syriac Christianity to the Rise
of Islam* (Chico: Scholars Press, 1982).

[6]F. Rosenthal, *Die Aramaistische Forschung* (n. 4).

Aramaic).[7] In the 3000 years that Aramaic has been a *living* language, it has exerted enormous influence. As Franz Rosenthal has written recently, Aramaic

> . . . was the main instrument for the formulation of religious ideas in the Near East, which then spread in all directions all over the world. Some, such as the gnostic systems, dominated the spiritual world view for centuries and then lost their identities; others, the monotheistic groups, continue to live on today with a religious heritage, much of which found first expression in Aramaic. Less direct, but certainly not negligible, was the role of Aramaic in the other endeavors of the mind which constitute civilization, intellectual matters such as science and philosophy, and even art. . . . The Aramaic language preserved a good deal of what there was to save, with great and lasting cultural consequences.[8]

One small consequence illustrates the influence of Aramaic. The English word "Hebrew" is not derived from the Hebrew, which is *ʿibrî*. It is derived from the Latin *Hebraei*, a transliteration of the Greek *ʾEbraîoi*, a transliteration of the Palestinian Aramaic *ʿebrayâ*.[9]

This essay aims to illustrate the importance of Aramaic studies in a more substantial way, however, by reference to the book of Job. This book is best represented in three Aramaic versions: the Job Targum from Qumran Cave 11 (11QtgJob),[10] the official Targum of Job, and the Peshiṭta of Job.

The last of these, the official Syriac translation, has appeared in several printed editions, the earliest of which is the so-called Paris

---

[7]On modern Aramaic, see D. Cohen, "Neo-Aramaic," *Encyclopaedia judaica* 12 (Jerusalem: The Macmillan Co., 1971) 948-952; K. Tsereteli, "Zur Frage der Klassifikation der neuaramäischen Dialekte," *Zeitschrift der deutschen morgenländischen Gesellschaft* 127 (1977) 244-253.

[8]F. Rosenthal, "Aramaic Studies During the Past Thirty Years," *Journal of Near Eastern Studies* 37 (1978) 82.

[9]R.A. Bowman, "Arameans, Aramaic, and the Bible," *Journal of Near Eastern Studies* 7 (1948) 88.

[10]There are also two targum fragments of Job 3:5-9 and Job 4:16-5:4 from Qumran Cave IV (4QtgJob). See J.T. Milik, "Targum de Job," *Discoveries in the Judean Desert IV, Qumrân Grotte 4, II* (Oxford: Clarendon Press, 1977) 90, plt. 28:157.

Polyglot of 1645. A new edition of the Peshiṭta of Job by the late
L.G. Rignell has just been published under the auspices of the Peshiṭta
Institute of Leiden.[11]   In a preliminary statement in 1973, Rignell
characterized the Peshiṭta of Job and commented on several previous
studies of the text.[12]   In general, these studies have suffered because
scholars have been unable to deal with the various manuscripts of the
book. The new edition should remedy that situation and the Syriac
version will then be able to take its place—indeed, create a place—in
unravelling the mysteries of the text and interpretative tradition of the
book of Job.

Similar remarks apply to the official Targum of Job. It too has
been printed in several editions, though none is entirely reliable.[13]   The
work of the late Raphael Weiss has contributed significantly to
establishing reliable controls for this targum and its manuscripts.[14]   His
intention was to produce the much needed critical edition, work which
has since been taken up by J. Fernandez-Vallina to appear in the
Madrid Polyglot.[15]   Until Fernandez-Vallina's work appears, scholars
can only take note of Weiss' general conclusions that the official
Targum of Job is a collection of different targums from different
periods. We must wait until a critical edition appears. Therefore, the
study that follows will not make a great deal of use of either of these
versions. Happily, the situation is different with regard to 11QtgJob.

---

[11]L.G. Rignell, *Job, The Old Testament in Syriac*, II, 1a (Leiden:
E.J. Brill, 1982).

[12]L.G. Rignell, "Notes on the Peshiṭta of the Book of Job," *Annual
of the Swedish Theological Institute* 9 (1973) 98-106.

[13]See remarks on this targum in relation to 11QtgJob by J.A.
Fitzmyer, *A Wandering Aramean* (n. 4) 167-175. The most accessible
text is that of P. de Lagarde, *Hagiographa Chaldaice* (Lipsiae, 1873);
reprinted (Osnabrück: Zeller, 1967).

[14]R. Weiss, *The Aramaic Targum of the Book of Job* (Tel-Aviv: Tel-
Aviv University, 1979), (in Hebrew with English summary).

[15]See the review of R. Weiss (n. 14) by F. Garcia-Martinez in
Journal for the Study of Judaism 11 (1980) 233.

Two excellent editions of the MS have appeared. The *editio princeps* in 1971,[16] and the edition by Michael Sokoloff in 1974.[17] In addition, individual studies of the text number nearly a hundred.[18]

The following, therefore, will concentrate on 11QtgJob: first, by looking back to the Hebrew text that the translator had before him; and second, by looking forward to the stream of tradition of which this targum is the earliest exemplar. In this way, it is hoped, one can appreciate the importance of the Aramaic Job.

I.

In spite of the fact that it has been observed that 11QtgJob provides "no substantive support"[19] for emending or transposing the received Hebrew text (MT), Ernest G. Clarke has shown that difficult

---

[16]J.P.M. van der Ploeg and A.S. van der Woude, *Le targum de Job de la grotte XI de Qumrân* (Leiden: E.J. Brill, 1971). For reviews, see J.A. Fitzmyer and D.J. Harrington, *A Manual of Palestinian Aramaic Texts* (Rome: Biblical Institute Press, 1978) 195.

[17]M. Sokoloff, *The Targum to Job from Qumran Cave XI* (Ramat-Gan: Bar-Ilan University, 1974). For reviews, see J.A. Fitzmyer and D.J. Harrington, *A Manual* (n. 16) 197; M. Dahood, *Biblica* 57 (1976) 269-270; P. Grelot, *Revue de Qumran* 9 (1977) 268-271; T. Muraoka, *Bibliotheca orientalis* 35 (1978) 318-322; S. Segert, *Journal of the American Oriental Society* 98 (1978) 145-146; G. Wanke, *Zeitschrift der deutschen morgenländischen Gesellschaft* 129 (1979) 349-350.

[18]See J.A. Fitzmyer and D.J. Harrington, *A Manual* (n. 16) 194-197; E. Kutsch, "Der Epilog des Hiobbuches und 11 QTG Job," *Zeitschrift der deutschen morgenländischen Gesellschaft, Supplement* 3 (1977) 139-148; R. Vasholz, "Two Notes on 11 Q tg Job and Biblical Aramaic," *Revue de Qumran* 10 (1979) 93-94; idem, "A Further Note on the Problem of Nasalization in Biblical Aramaic, 11 Q Tg Job, and 1 Q Genesis Apocryphon," *Revue de Qumran* 10 (1979) 95-96; E.G. Clarke, "Reflections on Some Obscure Hebrew Words in the Biblical Job in the Light of XI Q TG Job," *Studies in Philology in Honor of Ronald James Williams*, ed. G.E. Kadish and G.E. Freeman (Toronto: SSEA Publications, 1982) 17-30.

[19]M. Dahood, "Northwest Semitic texts and textual criticism of the Hebrew Bible," *Bibliotheca ephemeridum theologicarum lovaniensium* 33 (1974) 16.

textual problems can be illuminated by 11QtgJob.[20]   Another example
may be found in 11QtgJob 5:3-4, which is a translation of Job 21:22.
The Hebrew reads:

הלאל ילמד דעת והוא רמים ישפוט

There are two ways to translate this passage.   If one interprets
the second stich as a circumstantial clause, one may translate, "Will
any teach God knowledge, [seeing that] he judges those that are on
high?"   If one interprets the second stich as a parallel to the first, one
may translate, "Will any teach God knowledge, [seeing] He judges on
high?"[21]

Several scholars have tried to resolve the ambiguity by emending
the word רמים.   Thus, in support of the first alternative, Bernhard
Duhm amended the final *mêm* of רמים to an *hē*, reading **rĕmiyyah*,
"deceiver."[22]   The verse would be translated, "Will anyone teach God
knowledge, seeing that he judges a deceiver?"   There are difficulties
with this emendation, especially when one takes into consideration the
evidence of the Greek, but Duhm was close to the suggestion to be
made below.

In support of the second alternative, Mitchell Dahood contended
that the word רמים   refers to God himself.[23]   He translated, "Will he
teach God himself knowledge, and will he judge the Most High?"   This
translation takes the first *lamed* of הלאל as a *lamed* of emphasis, and
the final *mêm* of רמים as enclitic.   The consonants must also be
emended to רמם*   instead of רמים.   This emendation is clever, but
not satisfactory, for several reasons.   First, the elimination of the *yod*
has no support in the versions.   Second, as H.H. Rowley has pointed

---

[20]E.G. Clarke, "Reflections on Some Obscure Hebrew Words in the
Biblical Job in the Light of XI Q TG Job" (n. 18).

[21]For discussion, see R. Gordis, *The Book of Job: Commentary, New
Translation and Special Studies* (New York: Jewish Theological
Seminary of America, 1978) 232.

[22]B. Duhm, *Das Buch Hiob* (Freiburg: J.C.B. Mohr, 1897) 111.

[23]M. Dahood, "Some Northwest Semitic Words in Job," *Biblica* 38
(1957) 316-317.   See also M.H. Pope, *Job* (Garden City: Doubleday &
Co., Inc., 1965) 145-146; 3rd rev. ed. (1973) 160.

out, the suggestion is too strained, since the word הוא "he" is emphatic
and this normally would not be equated with the unexpressed subject of
the first line.[24]   Third, nowhere else in the Biblical text does the word
רמים refer to God.[25]

At first glance, the Septuagint and 11QtgJob seem not to offer
much help. In the Septuagint, we read the following:

$$\pi\acute{o}\tau\epsilon\rho o\nu \; o\dot{v}\chi\grave{\iota} \; \dot{o} \; \kappa\acute{v}\rho\iota\acute{o}\varsigma \; \dot{\epsilon}\sigma\tau\iota\nu \; \dot{o} \; \delta\iota\delta\acute{a}\sigma\kappa\omega\nu$$
$$\sigma\acute{v}\nu\epsilon\sigma\iota\nu \; \kappa\alpha\grave{\iota} \; \dot{\epsilon}\pi\iota\sigma\tau\acute{\eta}\mu\eta\nu;$$
$$\alpha\dot{v}\tau\grave{o}\varsigma \; \delta\grave{\epsilon} \; \varphi\acute{o}\nu o\nu\varsigma \; \delta\iota\alpha\kappa\rho\iota\nu\epsilon\tilde{\iota}.$$

"Is it not the Lord who teaches understanding
and knowledge? And does he not judge murderers?"

The Septuagint translated Hebrew רמים by $\varphi\acute{o}\nu o\nu\varsigma$, "murderers,"
from $\varphi\acute{o}\nu o\varsigma$, "blood."   The translator, it is usually thought, read the
resh as a *daleth*, taking the word to be *דמים.

In 11QtgJob 5:4 we read:

ו[ה]וא רמיא מדין אב°]

11QtgJob translated Hebrew רמים by רמיא . This has been
taken by all commentators to mean "the lofty [or haughty] ones," from
the Aramaic root רום , "be on high." רמיא , however, is a homograph
in Aramaic.   It can be a form of רום (Hebrew רום), or a form of

---

[24]H.H. Rowley, *Job* (London: Nelson, 1970) 189.

[25]In the MT , רמים occurs seven times, including the passage under
discussion.   In 2 Sam 22:28, it refers to the proud or haughty; in Ps
78:69, it may refer to the heavens since it is contrasted with earth; in
Isa 37:16, it may refer to a dwelling place.   Elsewhere (Deut 12:2, Isa
2:13,14), it refers to mountains or trees which are high, always with the
definite article.   In non-Biblical Hebrew, it refers to the elevated (*Num.
Rab.* 20:19), the exalted (*b. Ketub.* 103b: note variation בדמין) and
to the proud or haughty (*Midr. Ps.* 18:28).   The Aramaic evidence is
scarce.   The word does not appear in Biblical Aramaic.   In the
Targums, see Prov 25:3 "height," 6:17 "haughty;" Deut 28:52, "high,"
etc.   In non-Biblical Aramaic, it refers to mountains (*Gen. Rab.*, 32:10;
Cant. Rab. 14:4).

רמי (Hebrew רמה), meaning "to throw," "put on," "impose," "deceive."[26] Clearly, this last meaning would fit the context, as Duhm suggested long ago.

From this, it appears that two errors must be postulated, one on the part of the Septuagint (*daleth* for *resh*) and another in the *textus receptus* (*mêm* for final *hē*). Such a sequence is a possibility, though the compounding of errors in this way stretches the imagination. Another possibility is to take seriously the Septuagint reading of "murderer." In order to do this, one must examine the Hebrew word דמים , no small task because it may be derived from a variety of roots, all of them weak roots.[27] The roots are as follows:

דם	blood
דמה I	to be like (fail[28])
דמה II	to cease (to be quiet)
דמם I	to be silent, dumb
דמם II	to weep, wail, moan
דום	to stand still[29]

These roots, all found in biblical Hebrew, are found as well in cognate languages with similar meanings.[30] Sorting out the various meanings can be done only from the context.

---

[26]See for example, Targum Pseudo-Jonathan of the Pentateuch: רום in Gen 7:19, 14:6; Num 21:19 (twice), 21:20; Deut 12:2, 28:52; and רמה in Gen 35:6; Num 7:9 and 9:6.

[27]A. Baumann, "*dāmāh* II," *Theological Dictionary of the Old Testament* 3, ed. G. Botterweck and H. Ringgren (Grand Rapids: William B. Eerdmans, 1978) 260-265; F. Brown, S.R. Driver, and C.A. Briggs, *A Hebrew and English Lexicon of the Old Testament* (Oxford: Clarendon Press, 1962) 196-199.

[28]G.R. Driver, "Problems in the Hebrew Text of Job," *Vetus Testamentum Supplements* 3 (1955) 87, n. 1.

[29]G.V. Shick, "The Stems *dûm* and *damám* in Hebrew," *Journal of Biblical Literature* 32 (1913) 219-243.

[30]A. Baumann, "*dāmāh* II," (n. 27) 261.

In the Hebrew Bible, there are thirty-five occurrences of the word-form דמים. The word is usually taken to mean "blood" from דם . There are some instances, however, in which this meaning does not contribute significantly to the context. In several cases, the phrase "men of דמים" (i.e., "murderers"), is paralleled with the wicked (Psalms 59:3, 139:19; Proverbs 29:10), or is associated in the context with the telling of lies (Psalms 5:7, 55:24) or with those who take bribes and perform evil practices (Psalm 26:9). In some instances, the דמים are contrasted with those who speak uprightly and those who dwell on high (Isaiah 33:15,16). In all cases, the word דמים is clearly a synonym for the wicked, lying, and bribe-takers, as opposed to those who speak uprightly. In late Hebrew, the word דוד and its by-forms דודי and דמי have the sense of "evil report," or "speaking in a low voice."[31]   One may postulate, therefore, that דמים can be also a participial form from a root דמם III, "to be wicked," "deceiving," perhaps related to Ugaritic *dmm* "to abuse."[32]

It is possible, therefore, that the translators of the Septuagint and 11QtgJob both had a Hebrew text which read *דמים   and not רמים . The writer of the Septuagint translated by φονους, "murderer," perhaps because he was unaware of the meaning "deceive." The writer of 11QtgJob chose to translate the Hebrew by the Aramaic word רמיא "to be wicked." The Hebrew would then be translated "Will any teach God knowledge, seeing that He [God] will judge the deceiving one[s]?" This also fits the sense of the whole chapter.

If the above suggestions are correct, 11QtgJob illustrates an error in the *textus receptus*, the well-known interchange of *daleth* and *resh*. The Greek writer mistranslated, but the Hebrew copyist mistranscribed.

II.

A second area to which the Aramaic Job makes a contribution is the history of ideas, especially but not exclusively, the history of the

---

[31]M. Jastrow, *A Dictionary of The Targumim, The Talmud Babli and Yerushalmi, and The Midrashic Literature* (New York: Jastrow Publishers, 1967) 286.

[32]C.H. Gordon, *Ugaritic Textbook* (Rome: Pontifical Biblical Institute, 1965) 385.

religious ideas of Judaism and Christianity.[33]   An example of this
contribution is found in 11QtgJob 33:8 (=MT 39:27).   We read there,
או על מאמרך יתגב[ה] , "is it at your command that [the eagle] goes
up?" which is a literal translation of the Hebrew.   The interesting word
is the word "command," which the Aramaic translator wrote as מאמרך .
This is found also in the official Targum of Job.   Both targumists
translated the Hebrew idiom על פה meaning "command" by מאמרך, the
Aramaic word meaning "command."   This is not in itself particularly
significant.   What is significant is the fact that in later targumic usage,
the word מימרא is used extensively in other ways, and indeed has been
the subject of numerous studies.[34]   11QtgJob sheds important light on
this issue.

The debate concerning מימרא is over one hundred years old and
rests in part on the issue of whether Jewish and/or Christian literature
is anthropomorphic or anti-anthropomorphic.   Is there an attempt on
the part of the targumists to use מימרא in such a way that
anthropomorphic notions in the MT are avoided or eliminated?

If one looks at the targums of the Pentateuch, one finds that the
term מימרא is never used as a substitute for the tetragram or for
אלהים in the MT.   When these words occur in the Hebrew, they occur
in the targums.   However, מימרא is sometimes added to them.
מימרא also is used with pronouns referring to God's "self" in contexts
where God is speaking,[35] and as a translation of Hebrew קול "voice,"
and פה "mouth."   It is the use of מימרא for פה that is the concern
here.

Evidently, מימרא was used as a simple translation of the Hebrew
פה, whether of man or God in the earliest Aramaic translation
tradition.   In the instance of 11QtgJob 33:8 מימרא refers to Job's

---

[33]See E. Tuinstra, *Hermeneutische Aspecten van de Targum van Job
uit Grot XI van Qumran* (Groningen: 1971).

[34]For bibliography, see W.E. Aufrecht, "Surrogates for God in the
Palestinian Targums to Exodus," (Ph.D. diss., University of Toronto,
1979).

[35]W.S. Vorster, "The use of the Prepositional Phrase *bmymrᵓ* in the
Neofiti I Version of Genesis," in *De fructu oris sui: Essays in Honour
of Adrianus van Selms*, ed. I.H. Bayers and F.C. Fensham (Leiden:
E.J. Brill, 1971) 201-213.

"mouth" or "command," not God's. This use of מימרא for the human פה is found in Targums Onkelos and Pseudo-Jonathan of the Pentateuch,[36] as well as in the Samaritan Targum,[37] and the official Targum of Job. In the so-called Palestinian Targums, the situation is different. When the subject is the divine פה, the Aramaic phrase is always מימרא פום.[38] This suggests a tendency on the part of the Palestinian targumic tradition to make a distinction between the human and the divine פה: the phrase מימרא פום used to designate God's פה, and the word פום alone used to designate man's פה.[39]

This translation technique is seen more clearly with another so-called anthropomorphism, the word קול "voice" when applied to God. The Hebrew word קול is translated three times in 11QtgJob. In 34:5 (=MT 40:9), and 14:4 (=MT 29:10), Hebrew קול is translated simply by Aramaic קול. In 33:5 (=MT 39:25), the targum text is corrupt, but Hebrew קול is still translated by Aramaic קול. The subject in all cases is the human קול.

---

[36]There are twelve instances in both targums: Gen 43:7, 45:21; Exod 38:21; Num 4:27, 27:21a, 27:21b; Deut 17:6, 17:10, 17:11, 19:5a, 19:5b and 21:5. (מימרא in Onkelos only, in Exod 38:21; and in Pseudo-Jonathan only, in Num 4:27. In Exod 38:21, Pseudo-Jonathan reads פום מימרא.)

[37]A. Brüll, *Das samaritanische Targum zum Pentateuch* (Frankfurt: William Erras, 1876); A. Tal, *The Samaritan Targum of the Pentateuch, A Critical Edition, Part I, Genesis, Exodus* (Tel-Aviv: University Press, 1980); ibid., *Part II, Leviticus, Numeri, Deuteronomium* (Tel-Aviv: University Press, 1981).

[38]E.Y. Kutcher, *Studies in Galilean Aramaic*, trans. M. Sokoloff (Ramat-Gan: Bar-Ilan University, 1976) 20-22, 27, discusses the difference between פם and פום. He notes that פם is the Western form and that פום is the Eastern form. While this discussion is relevant for studying the language of the targums, it is beyond the scope of this short essay. Of concern here is the pattern of translation of the Hebrew פה. Therefore, the Aramaic word will be transcribed as פום throughout.

[39]The only exceptions which use פום מימרא of human פה are in Targum Neofiti (Deut 17:6, 21:5) and Neofiti Gloss (Exod 38:21, Deut 17:6 [gloss 2], 17:10, 19:5a [glosses 1 and 2], and 19:5b). On the probability of the Neofiti Glosses containing early translation traditions, see E.G. Clarke, "The Neofiti 1 Marginal Glosses and the Fragmentary Targum Witnesses to Gen. VI-IX," *Vetus Testamentum* 22 (1972) 257-265.

If one compares the Pentateuchal targums, one finds that there are fifty-three occurences in which קול refers to the human קול. In all but six occurrences, the targums translate by קול . In those six, the word מימרא is used, and these occur only in Targums Onkelos and Pseudo-Jonathan.[40] For these targums, מימרא can be used for a human voice. When, however, the subject is the divine voice, the word קול alone or מימרא plus קול is always used in all of the Pentateuchal Targums, even the Palestinian Targums. More importantly, the Palestinian Targums never use מימרא alone for the human voice.

Apparently, since God and man are not to be confused, it became necessary in translating to distinguish between the voice of man and the voice of God. The term מימרא, which was used initially as a simple equivalent of Hebrew קול, came to be used as a means of designating those passages which referred to God's voice alone. This is most fully and consistently developed in the Palestinian Targums, where מימראis used only in relation to the divine קול .

The tendency to use מימרא to translate only the *divine* פה and קול is the direction toward which the targumic translation tradition moved. The pattern of the מימראtradition shows that the Palestinian Targums should be located at the end point of targumic development. In their present form they are quite late.[41] The targumists were concerned initially with precision of translation, not the philosophic issue of anthropomorphism, and this so-called "buffer term" is not used to describe some creative, sustaining, or revelatory activity.[42] It is used, at least in these instances, only as a kind of marker to help the Aramaic-speaking audience distinguish between God and man when reading or hearing a translation of the Hebrew text.

----

[40]Gen 3:17, 16:2; Exod 18:24; Deut 21:18a, 21:18b, and 21:20.

[41]For identical conclusions on different grounds, see M. Allen, "The Palestinian Targum as Represented in Neofiti I with Reference to Selected Passages of Genesis," (Ph.D diss., University of Toronto, 1972), and the comments on Allen's work by A. Díez-Macho, "Neophyti 1. Textual Crystallization," *Neophyti 1, Targum Palestinense Ms de la Biblioteca Vaticana, V., Deuteronomio* (Madrid: Consejo superior de investigaciones científicas, 1978) 94*.

[42]J.A. Fitzmyer, *A Wandering Aramean* (n. 4) 95; M. Klein, "The Translation of Anthropomorphisms and Anthropopathisms in the Targumim," *Vetus Testamentum Supplements* 32 (1981) 162-177.

While this paper has been selective in its use of examples, there are numerous other illustrations to demonstrate the importance of the Aramaic Job. Presumably, further study of 11QtgJob and the Peshiṭta of Job will produce new insights. One eagerly awaits the new critical edition of the official Targum of Job to begin the same kind of study with, no doubt, similar results.

INDEX OF AUTHORS

INDEX OF SUBJECTS

INDEX OF TEXTS

New Testament

Rabbinic Literature

SR SUPPLEMENTS

1. **FOOTNOTES TO A THEOLOGY**
   The Karl Barth Colloquium of 1972
   Edited and Introduced by Martin Rumscheidt
   1974 / viii + 151 pp.
2. **MARTIN HEIDEGGER'S PHILOSOPHY OF RELIGION**
   John R. Williams
   1977 / x + 190 pp.
3. **MYSTICS AND SCHOLARS**
   The Calgary Conference on Mysticism 1976
   Edited by Harold Coward and Terence Penelhum
   1977 / viii + 121 pp. / OUT OF PRINT
4. **GOD'S INTENTION FOR MAN**
   Essays in Christian Anthropology
   William O. Fennell
   1977 / xii + 56 pp.
5. **"LANGUAGE" IN INDIAN PHILOSOPHY AND RELIGION**
   Edited and Introduced by Harold G. Coward
   1978 / x + 98 pp.
6. **BEYOND MYSTICISM**
   James R. Horne
   1978 / vi + 158 pp.
7. **THE RELIGIOUS DIMENSION OF SOCRATES' THOUGHT**
   James Beckman
   1979 / xii + 276 pp. / OUT OF PRINT
8. **NATIVE RELIGIOUS TRADITIONS**
   Edited by Earle H. Waugh and K. Dad Prithipaul
   1979 / xii + 244 pp. / OUT OF PRINT
9. **DEVELOPMENTS IN BUDDHIST THOUGHT**
   Canadian Contributions to Buddhist Studies
   Edited by Roy C. Amore
   1979 / iv + 196 pp.
10. **THE BODHISATTVA DOCTRINE IN BUDDHISM**
    Edited and Introduced by Leslie S. Kawamura
    1981 / xxii + 274 pp.
11. **POLITICAL THEOLOGY IN THE CANADIAN CONTEXT**
    Edited by Benjamin G. Smillie
    1982 / xii + 260 pp.
12. **TRUTH AND COMPASSION**
    Essays on Judaism and Religion in Memory of Rabbi Dr. Solomon Frank
    Edited by Howard Joseph, Jack N. Lightstone, and Michael D. Oppenheim
    1983 / vi + 217 pp.
13. **CRAVING AND SALVATION**
    A Study in Buddhist Soteriology
    Bruce Matthews
    1983 / xiv + 138 pp.
14. **THE MORAL MYSTIC**
    James R. Horne
    1983 / x + 134 pp.
15. **IGNATIAN SPIRITUALITY IN A SECULAR AGE**
    Edited by George P. Schner
    1984 / viii + 128 pp.
16. **STUDIES IN THE BOOK OF JOB**
    Edited by Walter E. Aufrecht
    1985 / xii + 76 pp.

EDITIONS SR

1. **LA LANGUE DE YA'UDI**
   Description et classement de l'ancien parler de Zencircli dans le cadre des langues sémitiques du nord-ouest
   Paul-Eugène Dion, O.P.
   1974 / viii + 511 p.
2. **THE CONCEPTION OF PUNISHMENT IN EARLY INDIAN LITERATURE**
   Terence P. Day
   1982 / iv + 328 pp.

3. TRADITIONS IN CONTACT AND CHANGE
Selected Proceedings of the XIVth Congress of the International Association for the History of Religions
Edited by Peter Slater and Donald Wiebe with Maurice Boutin and Harold Coward
1983 / x + 758 pp.
4. LE MESSIANISME DE LOUIS RIEL
Gilles Martel
1984 / xviii + 484 p.
5. MYTHOLOGIES AND PHILOSOPHIES OF SALVATION IN THE THEISTIC TRADITIONS OF INDIA
Klaus K. Klostermaier
1984 / xvi + 552 pp.
6. AVERROES' DOCTRINE OF IMMORTALITY
A Matter of Controversy
Ovey N. Mohammed
1984 / vi + 202 pp.

STUDIES IN CHRISTIANITY AND JUDAISM / ETUDES SUR LE CHRISTIANISME ET LE JUDAISME

1. A STUDY IN ANTI-GNOSTIC POLEMICS
Irenaeus, Hippolytus, and Epiphanius
Gérard Vallée
1981 / xii + 114 pp.

THE STUDY OF RELIGION IN CANADA / SCIENCES RELIGIEUSES AU CANADA

1. RELIGIOUS STUDIES IN ALBERTA
A State-of-the-Art Review
Ronald W. Neufeldt
1983 / xiv + 145 pp.

COMPARATIVE ETHICS SERIES / COLLECTION D'ETHIQUE COMPAREE

1. MUSLIM ETHICS AND MODERNITY
A Comparative Study of the Ethical Thought of Sayyid Ahmad Khan and Mawlana Mawdudi
Sheila McDonough
1984 / x + 130 pp.

Also published / Avons aussi publié

RELIGION AND CULTURE IN CANADA / RELIGION ET CULTURE AU CANADA
Edited by / sous la direction de Peter Slater
1977 / viii + 568 pp. / OUT OF PRINT

Available from / en vente chez:

Wilfrid Laurier University Press
Wilfrid Laurier University
Waterloo, Ontario, Canada   N2L 3C5

Published for the
Canadian Corporation for Studies in Religion/
Corporation Canadienne des Sciences Religieuses
by Wilfrid Laurier University Press